The Edge

Resume and Job Search Strategy

Third Edition

Bill Corbin and Shelbi Wright

jist
Publishing

The Edge Resume and Job Search Strategy,
Third Edition

©2000 by Bill Corbin and Shelbi Wright

Published by JIST Works, Inc.
8902 Otis Avenue
Indianapolis, IN 46216-1033
Phone: 1-800-648-JIST   Fax: 1-800-JIST-FAX
E-mail: editorial@jist.com   Web site: www.jist.com

Development Editor:	Lorna Gentry
Copy Editor:	Kristine Simmons
Project Editor:	Lori Cates
Cover Design:	designLab, Seattle
Interior Design:	Debbie Berman
Illustrations:	Brandon Corbin
Proofreader:	Gayle Johnson

Printed in the United States of America.

Cataloging-in-Publication data is on file with the Library of Congress.

03 02 01 00   9 8 7 6 5 4 3 2 1

ISBN: 1-56370-672-5

*"Retreating, hell!
We're just attacking
in a new direction!"*

———————————

U.S. Marine General O.P. Smith, 1950,
completely surrounded by a North Korean
army when a reporter commented,
"It looks like your army is retreating, General."

About the Authors

The Edge was conceived by Bill Corbin and developed by Shelbi Wright. Lorna Gentry revised the text for this third edition.

Bill Corbin is a 1968 graduate of the Harvard Business school. Early career experience includes stints at General Motors and RCA. In 1975, Corbin founded UN Communications, Inc., a printing/publishing enterprise. As a recipient of hundreds of job applications, Corbin became aware of the glaring inadequacy of most resume packages. As creative advisor to scores of clients, Corbin became convinced that a unique, dynamic job-search strategy yields results. The Edge Resume and Job Search Strategy represents more than 20 years of observation and experience in this field.

Shelbi Wright is a veteran of the employment recruiting field. A skilled researcher, Wright combined the best elements of conventional job-search strategy with the progressive wisdom of the Edge to make this book a complete package.

Lorna Gentry has worked in technical and reference publishing for over 10 years and has developed and edited a number of titles for such publishers as Que (Macmillan Computer Publishing) and Arco.

About This Book

Chapter 1: The Edge Philosophy and How It Can Work for You

In chapter 1, you learn about the Edge philosophy, you see how it has developed, and you learn how you can make it work for you in your resume preparation and job search. This information will be helpful to anyone entering or returning to the job market.

Chapter 2: Exploring Your State of Mind— and Formulating Your Career Goals

In chapter 2, you learn to recognize your strengths and to develop career goals that help you maximize those strengths. If you're considering a new career, you will find this information very helpful.

Chapter 3: Finding Opportunity

In chapter 3, you learn how, in an ever-expanding job market, you should take advantage of avenues other than the classifieds to find the right opportunities. Your journey begins here!

Chapter 4: Marketing Yourself Effectively

In chapter 4, you learn that selling yourself is the key—make sure your cover letter, resume, and follow-up system communicate the right message to potential employers. This important information pertains to anyone preparing to put the Edge to work in his or her job search.

Chapter 5: Creating the Perfect Cover Letter

In chapter 5, you learn how to really use the cover letter as an important opportunity to communicate your personal traits and values. Even if you've written cover letters before, you should take a moment to learn how the Edge philosophy applies to this important document.

Chapter 6: The Edge in Action: Sample Edge Resumes

Chapter 6 contains more than 25 examples of actual Edge resume and cover letter designs.

Chapter 7: Writing a Winning Resume

In chapter 7, you learn how to craft a resume that communicates the information and ideas that will get you the interview—and the job. You review the traditional techniques that still work, and you learn some new

CHAPTER 8

Creating Scannable and Electronic Resumes

Introduction

The job market is wide open. For every company that's downsizing or moving its operations to foreign soil, there's another company that's just opening its doors or undergoing unprecedented growth. The economy is booming, entrepreneurial enterprises are at an all-time high, and employers are scrambling to woo the right job candidates to their companies.

Within this burgeoning job market, your resume has never been a more valuable tool. With growing opportunity comes increasing potential for reward—for you, the employee. Your resume sets the stage on which you negotiate the best employment offer—a stellar salary, better benefits, greater potential for career advancement and promotion, and other qualities that make a career satisfying for you.

Even if you're not currently looking for a new job, one may be looking for you. Headhunters are combing the ranks of the employed, hoping to find good candidates who can be lured from their current positions by a better offer. If your resume is honed and waiting, you won't have to scramble to respond to offers that come your way. And you can even use an updated resume as a bargaining tool to upgrade your current job. An up-to-date, well-crafted resume can make the difference between having a job and managing a career.

"Ms. Smedley, if you're judging resumes on a per-pound basis, here's your man!"

The best news is that, despite popular opinion to the contrary, creating a winning resume doesn't have to be tedious, frustrating, or time-consuming. This book leads you through the process of crafting a well-tuned resume— one that captures the attention and respect of the reader and one that serves as your first step to that great job you've always dreamed of.

> "**E**ven if you're not currently looking for a new job, one may be looking for you."

How to Use This Book

This book covers a range of subjects, beginning with your state of mind and ending with a successful interview. However, two truths are important:

1. Many excellent reference books were written about the challenge of finding a job before this one came along. Some of them cover specific topics in more depth than is possible here. Throughout this book, we list references that provide additional help.

2. Depending on your career status, some parts of this book are more relevant to you than others. For example, the chapter about writing a resume draws heavily on traditional, proven concepts. If you are a first-time writer or your resume is badly outdated, this information will be helpful. If your word content is in good shape, you should concentrate on the sections that cover approaches to gaining a competitive edge.

Throughout this book, you'll find valuable ideas for making your resume rise above heavy competition. Even if your resume skills are excellent, the fresh ideas that the Edge brings to you can greatly improve your chances of getting the attention you deserve.

CHAPTER

1

The Edge Philosophy and How It Can Work for You

"This should give Ms. Smedley enough people to choose from."

after failing on previous attempts to secure an interview with a target company, sent them a shoe. His note: "I've been trying unsuccessfully for months to get my foot in your door, so I decided to try another approach. I truly believe my qualifications are ideal for your company. A resume is enclosed…." He got the interview.

We cover a variety of approaches—most less extreme than mailing shoes—to reach our primary goal: standing out in the very tall stack of applications for attractive jobs.

In the Beginning…: A Short History of Resumes and Their Development

History provides lessons we can learn from…or ignore and be doomed to repeat. It's worth our while to take a quick glance at how the common wisdom of resume crafting has evolved over the past few decades.

Prior to the age of word processing, most resumes were black-and-white affairs, designed to be plain, formal, and businesslike (in other words, completely lacking any reflection of the individuality or personality of the subject). They weren't fancy, but they met everyone's expectations, so they worked.

In the early '80s, we hit a recession and the job market tightened. The resume experts correctly determined that "because your resume is in tougher competition, you should do things to make it stand out." Their analysis was correct, and their two primary pieces of advice were the following:

1. Spend the money to have the resume professionally typeset.

2. Put it on ivory or gray paper.

As humble as these advances may seem, they set new standards for resume presentation and gave birth to the resume "industry."

The subsequent emergence of desktop publishing changed the resume game even more dramatically, by enabling almost anyone to create a highly designed and professional-looking resume. The stakes got higher as a move to ivory or gray paper became a less noticeable (and certainly less dramatic) resume upgrade, and many resumes came to reflect the "style over substance" mentality that was the hallmark of so much of American culture in the 1980s.

> **"S**omeday, you may need to adopt these techniques to be competitive. Now, you can adopt them to truly give yourself the Edge."

During the '90s, desktop publishing and quick printing became standard tools of the resume industry. As the decade progressed, most of the "rules" for resumes were tossed out, placing even greater demands on the resume writer's talent and creativity. Scanning technology has been integrated into resume screening processes in a large portion of the job market, heralding a reemergence of the black-and-white undesigned resumes of 20 years ago. Given the volatile nature of today's job market, everyone's a potential job candidate, so your resume is facing extremely stiff competition. Today's resume, when it sits in a pile 400 deep, needs both style *and* substance to really stand out to recruiters and potential employers.

Crafting a Resume for the 21st Century

This book makes the process of creating a striking, attention-grabbing, and impressive resume simple and understandable. We then develop a creative multi-phase job-search strategy, which will further distinguish you from "the crowd." Someday, you may need to adopt these techniques to be competitive. Now, you can adopt them to truly give yourself "the Edge."

A Note on Investment

We cover a variety of ways to secure real value for dollars spent on your job-search strategy. In general, however, creating a package that gives you a real Edge will cost more than typing your resume and making photocopies. You probably spent several years and tens of thousands of dollars to secure an education for Job #1. That you will need to spend a few bucks on your next job only makes sense.

CHAPTER

2

Exploring Your State of Mind—and Formulating Your Career Goals

"Thanks for participating in our profit improvement program, John!"

Some of you reading this book are doing so because you're considering a career change. You are comfortably situated at this time and are about to begin an orderly search for a better position. You are positive, confident, unhurried. You are also quite fortunate.

Other readers are on the other end of the spectrum. You were unexpectedly fired, laid off, or otherwise "restructured." The clock is ticking on your savings account. You (not to mention your loved ones) are moving from anxiety toward out-and-out fear. Your confidence is embattled, if not shot.

For some, the emotions of anxiety and fear are joined by an emotion very near grief. "The career that I thought would be 'for life' is unexpectedly over."

Tackling Work-Search Anxieties

Some emotional turmoil is a predictable, natural part of the job-search process. But it can do great harm to your ability to plan and execute an effective job-search strategy. Your thinking can be muddled. Your cover letters and interviews can sound increasingly desperate. In general, you just aren't a very pretty picture in the job market.

This book doesn't pretend to have answers to difficult emotional issues. But it does have the common sense to say this: If you are clearly embattled emotionally—if Roosevelt's famous "The only thing we have to fear is fear itself" has taken on a very personal meaning—you must take the time to tackle this issue first.

> "*If Roosevelt's famous 'The only thing we have to fear is fear itself' has taken on a very personal meaning, you must take the time to tackle this issue first.*"

If this book could fulfill its goals perfectly, you might find new confidence and direction in the Edge job-search strategy. However, you might need to patch a few leaks before setting sail. You may find answers in the support and counsel of your friends, in your faith, in support groups (which increasingly address the needs of those in the job-search project), in tapes or seminars aimed at self-confidence, or in the many books that specifically address this subject. Among the best known:

DuBrin, Andrew. *Your Own Worst Enemy: How to Overcome Career Self-Sabotage.* AMACOM, 135 W. 50th Street, New York, NY 10020. 1993.

Grappo, Gary Joseph. *The Top 10 Fears of Job Seekers: Your Guide to an Effective, Stress-Free Job Search.* Berkley Books, Penguin Putnam, Rockefeller Plaza, New York, NY 10020. 1996.

Hakim, Cliff. *We Are All Self-Employed: The New Social Contract for Working in a Changed World.* Berrett-Koehler Publishers, Inc., 450 Sansome Street, Suite 1200, San Francisco, CA 94111-3320. 1995.

Sack, Steven Mitchell. *Getting Fired: What to Do If You're Fired, Downsized, Laid Off, Restructured, Discharged, Terminated, or Forced to Resign.* Warner Books, 1271 Avenue of the Americas, New York, NY. 10020. 1999.

What Kind of Job Do You Want?

By definition, introspection is a very personal process—one that requires you to look into your own mind, to observe and analyze the dreams, desires, and feelings you hold for your life...and your career. There are no right answers. It's even difficult to find the right questions.

But this process is absolutely crucial to anyone beginning a job search. If you are "successful" in finding a job but spend the next several years being miserable about its requirements, income, or location, the job search certainly doesn't deserve to be called successful.

More positively, introspection can lead you to explore entirely new career fields. For example, veterans of traditional companies might consider opportunities in the nonprofit sector, or those who have always worked in a particular industry might consider transferring their skills to another industry.

Ask Yourself the Important Questions

Use your introspection to help define what types of work you want to do and in what type of industry and working environment you want to do that work.

First, ask yourself broad questions such as

- What are my skills?

- What do I like to do?

- What do I hate to do?

- What jobs fit my skills and desires?

- What are my practical needs for cash?

- How much adjustment am I willing to make to redirect my career?

  ▶ Change of responsibility?

  ▶ Development of new skills?

  ▶ Reduction of income?

  ▶ Relocation?

- Are my loved ones comfortable with my direction?

Then, at a more detailed level, factor in

- Bonuses? Stock options? Perks?

- Leadership? Management or staff member? Authority or subordinate?

- Prestige? Important title? Impressive company?

- Variety? Many or few responsibilities? Constantly changing or never changing functions? Similar days or different days?

- Advancement opportunities?

- Challenge on the job? Or familiarity with what you do and what's expected of you?

- On-the-job learning and training?

- Independence?

- Job security? Or a volatile position, department, or company? Easy commute? How long am I willing to travel to get to work?

- Flexible hours? Structured hours?

- Interaction with coworkers? Prefer to work with others or alone?

> *"At the very least, you should list those factors that are most important to you and then compare the list to the factors of the jobs you're considering."*

- Contribution to society? Directly or indirectly?

- Long-term or short-term employment? Retire with this company? Or is it just a rung on your corporate ladder?

- Company size? Large or small? Local, national, international?

- Personal office? Amenities?

- Travel? How many days out of the year? Daily, weekly, monthly? Locally, nationally, internationally?

At the very least, you should list those factors that are most important to you and then compare the list to the qualities of the jobs you're considering.

Several excellent books can help guide you through this process:

Bolles, Richard Nelson. *What Color Is Your Parachute? 1999: A Practical Manual for Job-Hunters & Career-Changers*. Ten Speed Press, P.O. Box 7123, Berkeley, CA 94707. 1998.

Sher, Barbara and Barbara Smith. *I Could Do Anything If I Only Knew What It Was: How to Discover What You Really Want and How to Get It*. Bantam Doubleday/Dell Publishing, Random House, 1540 Broadway, New York, NY 10036. 1996.

Tieger, Paul D. and Barbara Barron-Tieger. *Do What You Are: Discover the Perfect Career for You Through the Secrets of Personality Type*. Little, Brown and Company, Canada. 1992.

Other Resources for Career-Search Guidance

The Internet gives you access to a wide variety of career-search programs and information. You can find these sites by using any major search engine (Yahoo!, AltaVista, and so on) to conduct a search with the keywords "job search," "career planning," or even "jobs." In addition, a computer program called SIGI PLUS has been developed for college students as well as seasoned professionals. This detailed program helps prioritize your values and skills and then lists careers that correspond to your priorities. The program is distributed primarily through colleges and high schools but might be available in some public libraries.

If human guidance is helpful in your evaluation process, consider a career counselor. The effectiveness of professional counselors varies widely, so it is probably best to work with someone referred by an associate.

A host of self-help groups has sprung up around the country, providing an opportunity for introspection via honest dialogue with others facing the same career challenges.

CHAPTER

3

Finding Opportunity

"You know, Mary, I'm afraid John may be carrying this networking idea too far."

In a perfect world, you would pour a cup of coffee, grab your red pen, peruse the Sunday classified section, and find the job that perfectly matches your skills and goals. But today, you really limit your possibilities when you take such a passive approach to your job search. This chapter covers *aggressive* and *imaginative* job-seeking action—the kind of action that pays the biggest dividends in a rapidly evolving job market.

Certainly, the classifieds are a source of opportunities. Study the local ads. Study the ads in cities to which you'd move for the right opportunity. Fire off your Edge marketing salvo (cover letter, resume, and follow-up material) and hope for the best. But rather than simply sit, wait, and hope, dive aggressively into other search avenues.

You'll find a helpful worksheet on page 162 called Edge Job Campaign Worksheet. Copy and use this form to plot your course from beginning to end.

Why You Need an Aggressive Plan

There are two important reasons for aggressive alternative action:

1. It's your best statistical chance of finding the best job—not just *any* job.

2. A lot of the best jobs never appear in the classifieds. Job hunters relying strictly on classified ads often experience mounting frustration, anxiety, and fear. As time passes without the hoped-for response, these emotions can lead to an attitude of helplessness and defeat. If you're in high gear—making calls, writing letters, and researching companies inside and outside your industry—the positive action gives you critical forward momentum.

First, be aware that you are in a very dynamic job market. In addition to growth opportunities, even the businesses that are in the process of scaling back are often looking for new talent. In fact, mergers and downsizing actually create opportunities.

Somewhere out there:

> *"**R**ather than simply sit, wait, and hope, dive aggressively into other search avenues."*

- An irate board of directors will fire the CEO and most of his fellow incompetents.

- Several embattled CEOs, hoping to avoid being fired by their boards of directors, will fire incompetent staff members.

- Several embattled staff members, hoping to avoid being fired by the CEO, will fire incompetent subordinates.

- Several people in your job category will resign, retire, die, or become incapacitated.

- Aggressive young companies will launch new divisions or product lines.

- Successful entrepreneurs will realize they can no longer do it alone and will start building a management staff.

- Nonprofit organizations will receive the grant they needed to start a new endeavor.

Your Three-Step Strategy

The difficulty, of course, is knowing who will have these opportunities and when. Your strategy must be

1. Aggressive study

2. Timely communication of your skills, preferably in advance of the moment the opportunity actually occurs

3. Continuing follow-up as opportunity occurs

Doing Your Research

Mentally, you must be in constant research mode. Devour the local news, major newspapers, and any business-oriented publications that carry relevant information. Read every item with the mind-set: "What does this mean in terms of job opportunity?" As you zero in on specific job opportunities, make every effort to get closer to that organization.

Study and organize every available piece of information you can find on the company. Refer to the box on page 19 and the Company Research and Information Worksheet on page 163 for guidelines.

Using the Company's Web Site

Don't forget to check the company's Web site (often at the address www.*companyname*.com). Most companies maintain a site, where you can find job opportunities, company contacts, company history, recent press releases, and major products—all of the company's "for public consumption" information. Searching for the company's name in any of the various search engines (such as Yahoo!, AltaVista, and HotBot) will also lead you to articles and items written *about* the company by industry insiders. All in all, the Web offers one of the best information sources for your company research.

Trade Associations and Their Publications

Your Web research and library trips can yield the names of trade associations in your industry of preference. The publications of these associations (some are posted online) can provide valuable information on trends within specific companies. Every industry has multiple Web sites and several specialty magazines that carry the latest news on who is growing, launching new divisions, merging, going public, and closing.

Some Questions to Guide You in Company Research

1. How old is the organization?

2. What are its products or services?

3. Where are its plants, offices, or stores located?

4. Has the organization shown substantial and consistent growth?

5. What is its financial condition?

6. What are its new products or services?

7. Are there any plans for expansion?

8. Who are the company's primary customers?

9. Who are the organization's major competitors?

10. How does the organization rank in the industry?

11. What were the company's gross sales last year?

12. What is the organization's public image? Has it been in the media lately? Is there any public speculation about the company being involved in an upcoming merger or buyout?

13. To what degree is the organization committed to solving community problems? How has it contributed to the community?

14. Does the company have excessive employee turnover or other unusual organizational traits?

15. How centralized is the organizational structure? Do subordinates participate in decision-making activities?

Among the sources: *Standard and Poor's*, *The Thomas Register*, *The National Job Bank*, and *The Directory of Directories*

Incorporating Networking into Your Plan

Another vital action step involves that overworked buzzword of the '90s: "networking."

In addition to communicating your availability to friends, neighbors, and associates, try these creative networking techniques:

- Communicate with every professional contact on your Rolodex wheel.

- Ask your relatives and close friends for access to their network of friends, business associates, and contacts.

- Become active in local clubs or organizations, especially those geared toward your profession of choice or interest.

- Reconnect with old high school or college friends.

- If applicable, reconnect with former teachers or school administrators.

The Networking Contacts Worksheet on page 164 will help you organize the information you gather during your search.

Broadening Your Scope

Don't limit your networking activities to those people and businesses that fit into a strict job category. If you limit your scope, you limit your opportunities. A recent Edge client successfully jumped into an operations position in a national floral company. His previous stops had included operations positions in an electric motor company, a record/tape distribution company, and a

> *"Many hiring managers and recruiters are aware that skills are transferable among industries, and they are willing to consider those making a sizable career jump."*

20

national restaurant chain. Many hiring managers and recruiters are aware that skills are transferable among industries, and they are willing to consider those making a sizable career jump. If you have friends and associates who are really happy with their lines of work or the companies for which they work, talk with them about their careers. By networking creatively, you might find a new and satisfying career that wasn't in your original "plan."

Use Your Contacts Wisely

Communication with your network should be both verbal and written. A phone call might be useful in reestablishing contact, but verbal contact unsupported by written contact tends toward

> "Pete, John Miller here. You remember me… (fill in the years). Hey, Pete, I'm—as they say—'between engagements.' If you hear of anything that I might fit into, let me know, okay?"
>
> "Hey, sure, John—and great to hear from ya after all these years. Bye."

Pete, with no notes and only a temporary warm glow, is almost certain to forget the entire discussion by tomorrow morning. However, if he receives a supporting cover letter and resume within a couple of days, the odds of action increase dramatically.

Remember to communicate the proper role of your network. Pete does not need to be able to call you back in three days and say, "John, good news: You start next Monday at Acme Electronics." In fact, the burden of "finding you a job" will paralyze most people. You're simply asking that they advise you of

- Openings they become aware of

- High-potential situations they might know of

- Other networking sources for you to contact

If they can "put in a good word for you," that's great. If you can mention their names as referrals, that helps, too. But in general, you're simply asking for help in locating opportunities—not for help in actually landing the job.

Other Avenues of Opportunity

Don't limit your research and networking activities to any single "list" of recommendations. Think creatively and use any opportunity that arises. And, by all means, follow up on the information you uncover. If acquaintances work at a company in which you're interested, pump them for any relevant information and contact names. If possible, arrange an informational interview with one of their managers (as discussed in the next section). Prepare a cover letter that demonstrates your unusual degree of interest and knowledge. Forward your resume, hand-carried by an acquaintance if possible, to the key decision-maker.

The following sections outline some of the ways that you can uncover information and make important contacts that will help you in your job search.

Informational Interviews

The informational interview can be an excellent door opener. You are asking for perhaps 20 minutes of a manager's time to learn more about his or her industry, company, and job position. Some people will turn down requests for interviews, but a sizable percentage will be flattered by the request and will enjoy the opportunity to speak as an expert. Many companies are always on the lookout for new talent. Smart managers know that these interviews are a great way to identify potential candidates. From your standpoint, there are three major benefits:

- You learn more about companies that interest you and the jobs and people who make up those companies.

- You gain valuable interviewing experience—in effect from both sides of the desk.

- You might make the kind of contact and favorable impression that can lead directly to a job.

The most effective way to arrange an informational interview is through someone within your network. If this isn't feasible, forward a letter explaining your interest, and follow up by phone. A well-prepared list of questions and attentive note-taking are important parts of presenting a professional image.

Here are some useful questions to ask during the informational interview:

1. What are your responsibilities and duties? Can you give me some examples of your responsibilities and duties?

2. What happens during a typical workday in your position?

3. What do you like about your job?

4. What do you dislike about your job?

5. What do you like about this industry?

6. What do you dislike about this industry?

7. How did you get into this field?

8. What skills, qualifications, and other credentials are essential to being hired for this position?

9. What courses should I take, books should I read, or other experiences should I gain to prepare more fully for this type of work?

10. What type of training is available in this industry?

11. What advancement opportunities exist?

12. What is the salary range for employees in this field, and how do the salaries progress over the long term?

13. What will be the future trends in this field?

14. Who are your major competitors?

15. What sets your organization apart from your competitors?

16. What personal characteristics do you perceive to be critical to success in this field?

17. What is the typical career path for someone in this field?

18. What types of professional journals, trade publications, or other sources should I use to keep up with the trends and developments in this industry?

Try to be relaxed during the interview, and make sure you really listen to the things the person is saying. Even though the impression you make during the interview might lead to opportunity within the company, you don't want to appear as though angling for that opportunity is your sole purpose.

One Edge associate conducted extensive research on pharmaceutical companies. She contacted the sales managers of the top five firms who were selling in her city. All five agreed to spend 20 minutes answering her questions and were impressed enough with her knowledge of their field that she received three opportunities to interview within the companies.

Small Business Observational Visits

A variation on the informational interview is possible in some small companies. Ask the CEO for the opportunity to observe the operation and to make a report on your findings. If your insights and recommendations are impressive, you have an improved chance for any job openings.

Employment Agencies and Executive Search Firms

The yellow pages are a useful starting point regarding agencies specializing in locating jobs in your profession. However, be aware that companies vary significantly in effectiveness—so make every effort to research the success ratio of prospective firms. Most search firms derive their income from the employers. Unless you have specific information to make you think otherwise, you should avoid most organizations that charge *you* a fee. It's a job hunter's market today, and you rarely are asked to pay a headhunter's fee. If you are considering paying the fee, be very aware of all costs and the benefits that are promised.

Temporary Agencies

If you are currently unemployed, temporary agencies might provide income, momentum, and an avenue inside your companies of choice. (Again, the yellow pages are a source, but you should research agency effectiveness.) Most importantly, if you are exploring a new career area, temping can give you an opportunity to "test the waters" in a number of related organizations before you make a long-term commitment.

Consulting and Project Work

An alternative to interim employment is consulting or project work. Your research or your network might suggest opportunities to help companies who are expanding or companies who are struggling. You offer to join their team on an independent contractor basis. You sell the benefit that they can complete key projects without committing to a full-time hire. While on the job, you can determine whether the company is your kind of place in a career sense. If so, you can attempt to parlay the opportunity into a position.

Consulting is one of today's fastest-growing employment trends because it provides benefits for both the consultant and the hiring company. The consultant gets the freedom of working for a number of companies, on his or her own schedule, with the potential for unlimited income. The company benefits from the contractor's skill without taking on the long-term responsibility for that person's permanent employment—and employee benefits.

In addition to the many benefits of consulting, this career option has some drawbacks as well, such as less stability, lack of employer-paid benefits, and so on. To learn more about consulting, check out some of the many recent publications on the topic, such as

Bond, William. *Going Solo: Developing a Home-Based Consulting Business from the Ground Up*. McGraw-Hill, Inc., 11 West 19th Street, New York, NY 10011. 1997.

Holtz, Herman. *The Concise Guide to Becoming an Independent Consultant*. John Wiley & Sons, Inc., 605 Third Avenue, New York, NY 10158-0012. 1999.

Ludden, LaVerne L., Ed.D. *Be Your Own Business!: The Definitive Guide to Entrepreneurial Success*. JIST Works, Inc., 8902 Otis Avenue, Indianapolis, IN 46216-1033. 1998.

One Edge associate, out of a job but still enjoying adequate severance resources, made a company this unusual offer: "I know you need to implement a new employee evaluation system. I'll undertake the project on this basis: If I handle it to your full satisfaction, you'll pay me a fair price. If not, you'll pay me nothing." His approach secured a consulting contract, and although he had originally hoped for a full-time job offer, he learned he was good enough at consulting to make his consulting practice a full-time career.

CHAPTER

4

Marketing Yourself Effectively

*"Marge, do we have any openings for guys who can
leap tall buildings in a single bound?"*

It might occasionally happen that when your brilliantly crafted cover letter arrives along with a "perfect" resume, the recipient says, "Eureka, I have found him/her!" and you're in. But it's not likely. More often, finding the perfect job requires that you spend some time and energy marketing yourself. The job-search process involves not one but two levels of marketing:

LEVEL ONE:

- Your resume and cover letter have to be good enough to survive the initial review of a basketful of resumes and cover letters.

- Of the handful of resumes and cover letters that survive the initial screening, yours have to be good enough to be among the few selected for an interview.

- If you're still in the running, your *level one* selling job was a success. (The purpose of this book is to greatly improve your *level-one* odds.)

LEVEL TWO:

- You chat, smile, dance, and sing (and never let them see you sweat) in order to convince the first interviewer or interviewing committee that you're worth sending on for subsequent interviews.

- You repeat this process through subsequent interviews (perhaps two or three) until you convince all interviewers that you're the best applicant for the job.

Chapter 11 covers some ideas and references on the interviewing process.

> "*Good marketing, at a minimum, involves a predetermined set of steps...however, flexibility can be equally important.*"

The Elements of a Good Marketing Strategy

Good marketing, at a minimum, involves a predetermined set of steps:

1. Research as much as possible.

2. Write a personal cover letter using and demonstrating knowledge you gained during research.

3. Forward the cover letter with a powerful, visually striking resume.

4. Follow up by phone in a few days.

5. Follow up with a clever card in a few more days.

6. Follow up again by phone.

However, flexibility can be equally important. Your research doesn't do you much good if you can't adapt your plan to maximize the opportunities uncovered by that research. For example:

- Your research shows that the resume will go directly to the hiring manager (instead of a human resources manager). You are able to learn something about the manager (favorite sports team, college attended, sense of humor, or appreciation of blunt, straightforward talk). You tailor your cover letter to use that knowledge.

- Your research shows that the resume will be scanned in human resources. Therefore, an additional level of marketing is involved to survive the first cut. Your cover letter stresses the kinds of qualifications and personal traits that clearly make you the kind of person the hiring manager will want to consider. Your resume contains all the buzzwords that your research has shown to be effective for this type of position. You may even consider two cover letters—one to the initial screener and one to the hirer. Typically, a phone call will secure enough information to guide your approach.

Customizing Your Job-Search Strategy to Fit the Opportunity

Often, flexibility includes knowing how to customize your resume and cover letter for the type of hiring manager and hiring process you'll be dealing with. One of our associates recently survived the screening of 1,200 resumes to become one of 10 interviewees. His commentary is loaded with wisdom: "First, a human resources clerk scanned the resumes for the best 200. These went to the human resources manager, who forwarded 30 to the hiring executive. I figured the time spent in the first screening might be 30 seconds. So I loaded the cover letter with reasons my qualifications matched their requirements. I used a version of my resume that emphasized the skills they were seeking. I'm pretty sure the cover letter alone got me through the first screening. Then, the strong resume led to an interview."

Using the Edge Philosophy

Visualize a continuum between these two extremes:

1. You hear about a job for which you're perfectly qualified. You not only fit the educational and professional requirements, but also you were recently publicized in a widely read worldwide industry magazine as "(*job title*) of the Year."

2. You are determined to make a major career change. You must convince someone that despite zero apparent qualifications, you are capable, bright, and a quick study and will make that person very happy if he will only take a chance on you.

In point of fact, your qualifications for every job you apply for will fall somewhere on this continuum. Your position on the continuum determines the marketing approach you must use to succeed; you must be prepared to vary your marketing approach accordingly. Our theoretically perfectly qualified

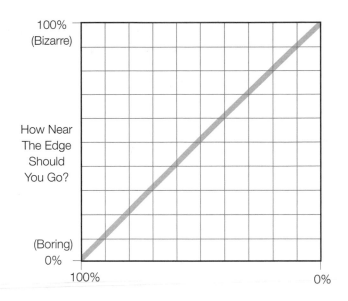

Your Percent of the Qualifications of
"The Perfect Candidate"

candidate can probably get the job by writing a two-paragraph letter announcing, "I am willing to join your firm. My requirements are…."

At the other end of the continuum is the cover letter of a graphic artist who, in order to overcome poor qualifications, wrote the following: "I know you'll see resumes with more formal job experience than I've had. But I also know I'm capable of quickly learning the job and accomplishing more than you presently think possible. To demonstrate my confidence, I'm willing to start at any wage you offer (including minimum) while I prove what I can do." She got the interview, got the job (at a reasonable starting wage), and accomplished everything she promised.

Let's pause to examine this woman's approach as an example of the Edge philosophy. Critics say, "You should never suggest you're less than fully qualified. You surely shouldn't say you're willing to work for a pittance." But those critics overlook this critical truth: The applicant was certain that she would not be as qualified as other applicants, and she knew that would be apparent from even a casual review of her resume. Based purely on the information on her resume, she anticipated that

she had zero chance of being hired. Therefore, she had nothing to lose and everything to gain by using a unique approach.

You must realistically assess your odds of securing the position. The worse your apparent odds are, the further toward the Edge you must move to have any practical chance of surviving the screening process.

On the other hand, if your qualifications are very strong, your goal should simply be a powerful, well-organized resume package that stands out graphically: clearly superior to the rest of the stack, but otherwise basically traditional.

Creating the Perfect Cover Letter

In achieving an Edge, your cover letter is at least as important as your resume.

Your cover letter should be

- Striking in appearance, with the same design theme as the resume

- Fully professional in content and presentation; carefully proofread to avoid grammatical errors, spelling errors, or typos

- Personalized to a name, not "To Whom It May Concern"

- Consistent with your marketing strategy:

  ▶ Experience-oriented if your experience is strong

  ▶ More unique and more values-oriented if your experience is not likely to be competitive with other applicants

The Mechanics of Your Cover Letter

The content of your cover letter is critical. But before you even begin to construct the content, you need to consider some important "mechanics" of your letter's construction: the technology you'll use to create the cover letter, the letter's addressee, and the size and stock of the paper and envelopes. Let's look at these issues in detail.

> *"If you have the right technology… you'll be amazed how much more dynamic your search process can be."*

Technology

You need access to modern word processing technology to produce your cover letters. By working with an electronic copy of your cover letter, you can easily personalize the addressee and edit the content to include information specific to the recipient.

Print quality must be excellent, and laser quality is best. If you don't have a printer, you can take a disk containing your letter to any quick-print service for an inexpensive, professional-quality printout. Many schools and libraries also have these printers available.

In general, strive to make "smooth, easy communication" a positive tool in your job search. Too often, people fail to get off an important letter simply because it's a hassle to get it typed. We've heard admissions that "I didn't mail that letter because I didn't have a stamp." If you have the computer technology—buy or rent it if you don't—and all the supplies that make communication easy, you'll be amazed how much more dynamic your search process can be.

Finally, you'll find that many jobs advertised online request that you send your resume and cover letter via e-mail. This technology makes the delivery of your materials very simple—but watch that you don't send anything without thoroughly proofing it first. Don't let the immediacy of e-mail lull you into sloppy communications. We talk more about preparing and sending electronic communications in later chapters of this book.

The Addressee

Even at considerable cost of online time, library time, or long-distance phone charges, invest in finding real names. A cover letter addressed to *personnel manager* or *human resources coordinator* or *to whom it may concern* is already less competitive. Although a few exceptions exist, accurate contact information is available to you in almost any situation. With the wealth of resources available to you for tracking down this information, you look downright lazy or uninformed if you don't include a real name on your cover letter.

The Size and Paper Stock of the Envelope

The two standard envelope sizes are #10, the standard business-size that involves tri-folding your contents, and 9 × 12 catalog envelopes, which can hold unfolded, standard-size ($8^{1}/_{2}$ × 11) paper.

The cost of the two alternatives might be surprisingly similar. If you select a #10 that matches the resume, the cost of this premium stock is relatively high. Plain white 9 × 12s cost only slightly more than #10s. As a third alternative, most companies make 9 × 12 envelopes in a variety of custom paper stocks, but these may carry a premium cost. Check with the supplier for availability and costs.

Under current postage regulations, the larger-size envelopes cost about 11 cents more to mail.

The best argument for the 9 × 12 is that your resume remains flat and is therefore slightly easier to read, stack, and file. Further, if your resume will be scanned (you learn more about scannable resumes in chapter 8), you must submit it flat and unfolded. If you're not submitting a scannable resume, this benefit might not outweigh the costs of purchasing and mailing the larger envelopes.

Premium envelopes that match your resume paper are expensive versus purchasing plain white #10s at the discount office supply store—which probably cost less than a penny each. Some argue that the envelope is ripped and pitched immediately; therefore, the cheapie is acceptable. Although this position is arguable, it is clearly not consistent with the Edge concept of creating a truly standout resume package. We conclude that a matching #10 envelope is worth the investment. Depending on the increased cost, the matching 9 × 12 might be worth the extra investment as well. However, if the resume is to be scanned, a white 9 × 12 will be fine; in most cases, the person opening and scanning the resumes won't be the hiring manager.

The Content of Your Cover Letter

At its most basic, this letter covers

- How you became aware of the opportunity or what led you to contact the company

- What you know about the company and the opportunity

- Some direct statement of what you can do for the company, such as how you can increase its profitability, move it toward its financial or organizational goals, or otherwise contribute to its success

- A direct request for an interview

Chapter 6 includes three complete cover letters. In several respects, the sample on page 47 represents the ideal cover letter. The hiring company had listed the qualifications it was seeking. The applicant had strong enough experience to confidently fill each need. The cover letter became a virtual "checklist" and was successful. This approach is usable unless you are so clearly stretching your relevant experience that the recipient begins chuckling as he "deep sixes" your package.

If you do not have knowledge of the specific job or qualifications a company is seeking, use your research to tie likely needs to your skills.

> "Because profit margins in the steel industry have been squeezed by foreign competition, it's clear that aggressive programs to cut costs and raise efficiency are vital. In the last three years, I have reduced the cost of goods sold by 4 percent through a combination of labor efficiencies and creative purchasing. I am confident my experience fits perfectly with your needs and look forward to discussing this job opportunity with you."

> "A mutual acquaintance, John Smith, filled me in on the competitive challenge you face since ABC Corporation moved into your primary marketplace. The possibility of significant loss of established customers is a threat to be addressed aggressively. Between 1995 and 1999, I served as Marketing Director in my company's Midwest region. We faced new competition from XYZ Corporation and implemented a powerful series of counterattacks, which resulted in a 2 percent increase in market share. I am confident…"

> "While studying your company in *The Wall Street Journal* and several trade publications, I became aware of the difficult strike situation you faced last year. Of course, the aftermath is always a period filled with conflict and morale difficulties. In 1998, I served as Corporate Communications Director, where I was directly responsible for rebuilding morale through a series of creative communication vehicles. I am confident…"

If your qualifications do not clearly meet the company's needs, you are faced with an interesting dilemma: Fib, or find another way.

The Benefits of Candor

Many resume writers resort to creative puffery. One writer admitted his phrase "worked closely with top management on evaluation of national ad campaign" was inspired by an elevator ride when the CEO casually asked what he thought of a new ad. Readers of resumes know the resume is probably puffed. ("If this person were really this good, she'd be president of her company instead of looking for a job.")

The Edge concept offers an important alternative: Candor coupled with expression of positive personal values can overcome shortcomings in resume qualifications.

To successfully market your personal values, you need to be aware of two crucial facts:

- Every experienced hirer knows that con artists can write good resumes. Some very qualified people can be nasty, lazy, insolent to superiors, brutal to subordinates, drunkards, liars, or thieves. Although we exaggerate a bit (for comic relief), it remains true: Technical job skills do not ensure a good employee; good employees must also have good personal values.

- Speaking frankly, it's important to be sure you have good values before you communicate them in your cover letter. If necessary, examine values such as your work ethic, your ability to work smoothly with people, and your ability to handle stress without losing your sense of humor. False communication regarding values might get you a job, but it won't help you keep it. The person hired as a hard worker will be fired as soon as he turns out to be a 3:30 p.m. golf junkie.

Here are some examples of values communication that can work in a cover letter:

"I'm well aware that in today's job market, you'll land people with more years of experience than I've had. But you won't land anyone willing to learn faster or work harder. I'll study and take classes on my own time. And I'll succeed in this job through a level of hard work and dedication to excellence that will serve as a positive example for other employees."

"A review of my resume will show I'm moving from a stagnant industry into your far more dynamic field. Therefore, my qualifications might not seem to directly apply. However, please be aware that I have directly managed a staff of _____ , have been accountable for a budget of _____ , and have demonstrated my versatility through successful stints as _____ , _____ , and _____ . I study hard and learn quickly. On the job, I ride hard, shoot straight, and never quit until the job is done. I'm confident you'll find my performance consistent with the commitment to excellence your company has made."

"Okay, I need a little extra help here. When you see my resume, you're going to say, 'Hey, this guy is too young, too green, or too something to be considered.' WAIT! STOP! DON'T PUT ME ON THE BOTTOM OF THE STACK! You'll be happy you gave me a little extra consideration.

"All my life I've succeeded by setting high goals and then working as hard as it takes to achieve them. I work extremely well with people. I learn fast and communicate well. I even accept criticism gracefully and take whatever steps are needed to fix what's wrong.

"Give me an interview. You won't be sorry!"

In some cases, particularly when applying for high-level leadership positions, how you communicate your values can be as important as how you communicate your experience.

"As an applicant for your vital leadership position, I'd like to step outside 'resume mode' for just a minute. I'm sure my job qualifications are competitive. I've been 'down the road' in the necessary areas of marketing, finance, manufacturing, and human resources. But I feel strongly that effective leadership has more to do with values than the length of a resume. I lead by example— by demonstrated hard work and commitment to excellence. I build an effective team the same way successful coaches build teams. We build pride through performance and performance through relentless execution of the fundamentals of our business. From all I know about your company, we share the same goals and the same commitment to excellence. I look forward…"

Using Humor

A strange void in the resume field is humor. A recent study of "bosses" determined that sense of humor is viewed as one of the single most important traits of employees. Yet humor is very rare and, used carefully, is a clear opportunity to execute the Edge philosophy. Why not a clever quote at the bottom of your cover letter or an appropriate cartoon printed on your envelope? We cover humor more in chapter 9.

> *"**H**ow you communicate your values can be as important as how you communicate your experience."*

CHAPTER

6

The Edge in Action: Sample Edge Resumes

The following pages represent samples of Edge resumes and cover letters "in living color." The contents of each resume have been "fictionalized to protect the innocent," but the words and formats might be helpful as you begin to write your resume.

Each resume was written by a member of the Professional Association of Resume Writers (PARW). Many of these individuals are also Certified Professional Resume Writers (CPRW). This designation signifies a member of PARW who has been tested and evaluated on his or her skills and techniques as a resume writer. (You can read more about PARW on pages 98–99.)

How to Use This Chapter

We recommend that you take a three-step approach to using the information and examples included in this chapter:

1. Do a quick thumb-through to gain an overall impression of the kinds of techniques that create an Edge resume.

2. Do a more detailed search for approaches that fit your personal style and career needs.

3. Work with your printer or resume consultant to develop and execute the chosen design.

You can use this section to stimulate your creative processes, leading to your own unique design. Or you can simply copy the ideas presented here. Be aware of the possibility that competitors have also read this book. For most designs, this represents no problem. For a design such as the teacher's apple with a quote on page 85, you should probably modify the concept to make your resume unique.

The cost of executing these ideas varies significantly. Some of the resumes can come from a desktop publisher and a quality copier. Others require the expertise of a strong commercial printer. Appendix A discusses the cost issues as well as the technical specifications for preparing each design.

You might want to study appendix A carefully. Or you might want to skim the cost information for an affordable design and let your printer wade through the technical details.

Contributing Resume Writers

We thank the professional resume writers who contributed their expertise by submitting their own resume examples. You can contact these professionals through PARW at 800-677-9090.

Contributing Writers

45	Betty Geller, CPRW, Apple Resume & Typing Service, Elmira, NY
47, 49	Mark Berkowitz, NCCC, CPRW, Career Development Resources, Yorktown Heights, NY
51	Margaret Lawson, Professional Resume Writer, New York City, NY
53 & 87	Dana K. Calhoun, CPRW, Superior Office Support, Inc., Clearwater, FL
55	Kate Phelon, CPRW, Parker, Phelon & Associates, Westfield, MA
57, 59	Gayle Bernstein, CPRW, Typing Plus, Indianapolis, IN
61	Judith Friedler, CPRW, CareerPro Resume Services, New York City, NY
63	Carol Lawrence, CPRW, A-Plus Office Services, Inc., Snellville, GA
65	Carole Warga, CPRW, Rocky Mountain Resume Company, Loveland, CO
67	Jonathan Evans, Career Support Services, Amherst, MA
69, 71	Beverley Kagan, CPRW, Beverley Kagan Resumes, North Miami Beach, FL

CPRW—Certified Professional Resume Writer

NCCC—Nationally Certified Career Counselor

NCRW—Nationally Certified Resume Writer

PLS—Professional Legal Secretary

JOSEPH MAXWELL

2442 North Parker Avenue
Liverpool, NY 13090
(315) 555-3418
jmaxwell@writeme.com

QUALIFICATIONS SUMMARY

- Extensive broadcast on-air, programming, and promotions experience
- Enthusiastic, motivated, results-oriented team leader
- Excellent writing, analytical, and creative abilities
- Active participant in civic and community projects
- Skilled multi-track production talent

PROFESSIONAL EXPERIENCE

Administrative / Management
- Oversaw all aspects of personnel and operations in broadcasting programming, production, and engineering.
- Worked in conjunction with sales and promotions departments to develop ongoing promotions/ marketing strategies to facilitate revenue building and listener awareness.
- Prepared frequent analysis reports for presentation to upper-level management on departmental strengths and areas of weakness needing attention.
- Developed relational database system to access large volumes of data for special project needs.
- Oversaw preparation and administration of annual departmental budget.
- Coordinated and managed reports for quarterly submission to federal government.

Supervision / Training
- Recruited, trained, and supervised personnel in broadcasting programming, news, and engineering.
- Conducted performance appraisals, particularly in areas where presentation skills were of critical importance.
- Encouraged and assisted staff in developing computer skills, which increased efficiency.
- Supervised weekly scheduling of all departmental personnel and time-off requests.
- Coordinated daily troubleshooting associated with programming and traffic departments.

Communications / Public Relations
- Designed and instituted first student intern program, allowing young broadcasters an opportunity to observe and participate in daily station operations.
- Promoted company's public commitment through participation in community service projects.
- Recognition and recipient of numerous citations for outstanding public service.

EMPLOYMENT HISTORY

1997–Present	Operations Director/Morning Personality	WTUI Radio—Syracuse, New York
1994–1997	Full-time Student	Columbia College
1988–1994	Operations Director/Morning Personality	WXIE/WNUR—Utica, New York
1977–1988	Afternoon Drive Personality	WPWC Radio—Syracuse, New York

EDUCATION

B.A., Business Management concentration, Columbia College
Communications major with concentration in Radio and TV, Ohio University

ROBERT LAWSON
345 River Avenue, #43
New York, NY 10031
(212) 555-1927

September 27, 1999

Ms. Ann Murphy
Director of Personnel
Victim Services
2 Lafayette Street
New York, NY 10007

Dear Ms. Murphy,

I am excited about your job posting for a Research Associate in your organization. This position has a strong appeal to me. Therefore, please accept this letter and accompanying resume as application for the Research Associate position.

With more than three years experience in the Child Welfare Administration, I have learned quite a bit about the day-to-day workings of the justice system.

Please allow me to highlight my skills as they relate to your stated requirements:

YOUR REQUIREMENTS	**MY EXPERIENCE**
✓ Ability to develop contacts with leaders of immigrant communities.	✓ Proven ability to work successfully with immigrant populations involved in the criminal justice and child welfare systems.
✓ Experience interviewing criminal justice officials.	✓ More than three years experience working with lawyers, probation and parole officers, and drug counselors.
✓ Ability to conduct focus groups of immigrants to elicit experiences with the criminal justice system.	✓ Served as president of a college association of immigrant students, conducting meetings about issues that affected the students.
✓ Degrees in social science or social service.	✓ Have both B.S. and M.A. in criminal justice.

As you can readily see, my background provides the skills that you require for this position.

I am accustomed to a fast-paced environment where deadlines are a priority and handling multiple jobs simultaneously is the norm. I enjoy a challenge and work hard to reach my goals. Constant negotiations have strengthened my interpersonal skills.

I look forward to speaking with you in the near future to schedule an interview at your convenience, during which I hope to share with you how I could best contribute to your organization.

Sincerely,

Robert Lawson

Robert Lawson

ROBERT LAWSON

345 River Avenue, #43
New York, New York 10031
(212) 555-1927

OBJECTIVE   A position as a Research Associate that will require strong interpersonal skills, knowledge of immigrant issues, and extensive training and experience in criminal justice.

PROFILE
- Motivated criminal justice professional with successful three-plus–year track record resolving cases involving both the child welfare and criminal justice systems.
- Organized, detail-oriented individual with exceptional follow-through abilities; demonstrated ability to effectively prioritize a broad range of responsibilities in order to consistently expedite case processing.
- Possess strong interpersonal skills; able to work effectively with individuals on all levels.
- Computer literate; expertise in using WordPerfect; extensive data-entry experience.

EDUCATION
May 1998
May 1994

John Jay College of Criminal Justice, New York, NY
Master of Arts: Criminal Justice
John Jay College of Criminal Justice, New York, NY
Bachelor of Science: Criminal Justice
Significant achievement: Served as president of the Caribbean Students Association.
- Coordinated activities to provide information for Caribbean students and conducted meetings concerning issues affecting Caribbean students and Caribbean immigrants in general.

EXPERIENCE
September 1996–
Present

Child Welfare Administration, New York, NY
Case Worker
- Coordinated and conducted meetings between clients and school officials.
- Maintained contact with lawyers, parole and probation officers, and drug counselors to expedite positive resolution of cases and ensure that clients attended counseling.
- Maintained contact with incarcerated clients to apprise them of relevant progress.
- Testified in both family and criminal courts.
- Monitored progress of children placed in kinship/foster homes to ensure a positive environment.
- Prepared and submitted progress reports indicating status of parents' readiness to take responsibility for children's care.

March 1995–
September 1996

Nycom, Inc., New York, NY
Telephone Operator
- Placed various types of operator-assisted calls.
- Tracked customer complaints.

June 1994–
March 1995

LD-OS, Inc., White Plains, NY
Telephone Operator
- Placed operator-assisted calls for customers.
- Tracked customer complaints.

December 1993–
June 1994

City Security Guards, Inc., New York, NY
Security Office
- Submitted daily general reports in addition to reports on any criminal or unusual occurrences.
- Ensured building security at midnight by closing and securing all entrance and exit doors.

June 1991–
December 1993

John Jay College of Criminal Justice, New York, NY
Student Aide: Data processing
- Handled data-entry duties for computerized information system.

Michael B. Olson

3264 Seventh Avenue #101
Seattle, WA 98808
(607) 555-0990
M_B_Olson@mymail.com

Objective

Bookkeeping Operations Supervisor

Qualifications

Highly organized and experienced in bank reconciliations, accounts payable / receivable, payroll, year-end account analyses, expense accounts, check writing, training, and supervision. Windows, Linux, Lotus 1-2-3, WordPerfect 9, MAI Basic Four.

Work Experience

Bookkeeper (Office Manager)
Triad Data Inc., Seattle, WA
1999–Present

- Computer consultant firm.
- Manage accounts payable for all branches throughout Texas, Europe, Atlanta, and Connecticut (over 100 relationships).
- Issue check disbursements for consultants, office sundries, payroll, vendors, rent as per lease agreement, etc.
- Balance expense accounts, including clarification of any discrepancies for 12 officials.
- Created computerized client files for easy tracking and posting.
- Closed out accounts at year end; opened new books at fiscal start.
- Constructed expense procedure manual. Used for reimbursement of all business expenses (i.e. travel, hotel, entertainment, relocation).
- Trained new personnel on computerized cash receipt program for more than 75 accounts.
- Appreciated most for efficiency and thorough stratagem.

Billing Manager
Camera Service Center, Inc., Seattle, WA
1994–1999

- Motion picture rental equipment firm.
- Controlled approximately $179,000 in billings for 500 clients:
  - Affirmed that clients were billed in accordance with established coding procedures.
  - Verified contract status and updated customer accounts on receipt of payments.
  - Discussed fee arrangements with upper management in relation to overdue accounts.
  - Assessed profits and losses at year end; closed files; ran sales journal; reviewed cash receipts.

Account Clerk
Seattle League for Hard of Hearing, Seattle, WA
1989–1994

- Agency offering assistance to those with hearing dysfunctions.
- Reported to controller.
- Night depository: checked day sheet and cash endorsements, prepared deposit slip; proved cash; verified identification; issued reimbursements; prepared report for Human Resources / City of New York.

Education

Lehman College, Bronx, NY	*(Accounting)*	*1997*
RCA—Financial Service Course	*(Certificate received)*	*1990*

"A PENNY SAVED IS A PENNY THAT GOES TO THE BOTTOM LINE."

DEBORAH I. LANE

2150 Briarwood Place, #B
Palmer, MA 34683
(813) 555-3100
DeborahL@mailaddress.com

SUMMARY

Project coordinator/consultant with extensive experience in the consumer service and telemarketing environments. Strong ability to analyze situations, recommend change, and implement new ideas.

Strengths:	Leadership, role model, team player
	Organization and follow-through
	Marketing and sales coordination
	Implementation of programs and procedures

PROFESSIONAL EXPERIENCE

Consumer Services Coordinator   2/95–Present
TAMBRANDS, INC., Palmer, Massachusetts

- Responsible for consumer problem-solving and ensuring consumer satisfaction.
- Coordinated and revised consumer response paragraph and letter libraries.
- Developed procedure for monitoring, and monitored an outside telemarketing agency.
- Systems administration for consumer response information systems (CRIS) codes.
- Consumer services department liaison with marketing and sales department in New York City.
- Attended monthly meetings to track and resolve current top-eight complaints.
- Consumer services department liaison with five fulfillment houses.
- Prepared correspondence regarding marketing promotions and product information inquiries.
- Developed reference manual for promotion. Kept managers/consumer reps informed of status.
- Member of cost-savings team. Team leader of department consumer service suggestions.
- Representative for Junior Achievement program. Conducted presentations to high school students.
- Conducted consumer education on use of diagnostic kit.

Volunteer Coordinator (Grant Position)   8/94–2/95
MONSON COUNCIL ON AGING, Monson, MA

- Community liaison bringing seniors and youth together.
- Maintained homebound outreach program and encouraged participation by new seniors.
- Created and implemented new programs.
- Recruited, trained, and scheduled volunteers.
- Public relations representative for senior center.

Sales Administrator   6/89–8/94
LIGGETT & MYERS TOBACCO COMPANY, Ludlow, MA

- Assisted regional manager with eight account managers.
- Coordinated data, conferences, and promotions.

EDUCATION

Springfield Technical Community College, Springfield, MA
Various courses, including computer applications and English composition.

Various seminars and programs on office management practices. WordPerfect and Word for Windows, EMT training, and consumer response information systems certification.

ANDREW E. FREEMAN

6119 Burlington Avenue
West Springfield, MA 01089
(413) 555-7554

ASSETS

Current Assets

Strong analytical and problem-solving skills with ability to establish, streamline, and automate accounting systems. Solid academic background in accounting that includes teaching at the collegiate level. Thorough and well-organized in completing projects; committed to professionalism.

Fixed Assets
- **M.S., Accounting,** Western New England College, Springfield, MA, in progress
- **A.S., Accounting,** Holyoke Community College, Holyoke, MA, 1997
- **B.B.A., Finance,** University of Massachusetts, Amherst, MA, 1991
*Self-financed 100% of college education through full-time employment.

Intangible Assets
- Prepared over 50 individual tax returns of various complexities.
- Completed worksheets for CPA to complete final business tax return.
- Tutored college students in Accounting I, II, Intermediate, Cost, and Managerial Accounting.
- Introduced new teaching methodologies at Holyoke Community College, which were adopted by instructors, mentors, and lab assistants.
- Analyzed and modified cash reconciliation system for multiple departments, as well as other municipalities, which increased efficiency. Individually cleared up five-month backlog.

LIABILITIES

Dividends Payable

Academic and real-world experience payable to employer.

EQUITY

Retained Earnings

Miscellaneous employment while pursuing M.S.A.   1998–Present

Holyoke Community College, Holyoke, MA   1997–1998
Adjunct Professor of Finance (Fall Semester, 1997)
"Principles of Financial Management" (Corporation Finance)

Accounting Mentor (1996–1997)
Lectured on Principles of Accounting I and II and provided relevant examples. Met with students one on one to provide tutoring as needed. Developed updated course proposal to reintroduce Principles of Financial Management.

Old Colony Envelope Co., Westfield, MA   1994–1995; 1986–1992
Papercutter:
Operated and maintained computer-controlled paper-cutting press. Introduced new methodologies, resulting in higher standards of quality and production efficiency.

The Phoenix, Greenfield, MA   1992–1993
Policy Change/Commissions Analyst:
Researched and audited agents' commission history to coordinate discrepancy resolutions and timely payments for major, multi-line insurance corporation. Designed, developed, and tested models for dividend ledger proposals on Lotus 1-2-3. Improved efficiency of the analysis of financial information and proper organization of data via effective computer use.

Sally Mitchell Klein
7181 North Cooper Street
San Francisco, CA 94112
(101) 555-3453

Helen Mitchell Young
3812 Crescent Drive
San Francisco, CA 94112
(101) 555-2445

March 18, 2000

Wendy Hudson
Education Director
Wellington Art League
1234 Jersey Street
San Francisco, CA 94110

Dear Ms. Hudson:

Two positions—one dynamic team! The positions of Fine Art Day Camp Director and Fine Art Day Camp Assistant Director are tailor-made for us, and together we can provide a cohesive missing piece to your Summer Camp's staff. Not only are our professional experiences and backgrounds similar, but we are sisters who are long-time cohorts and business partners and are positively creating "our mark" in the world of funky and fun art, the reputation of your institution.

We love what we do. And when we develop a project, we bring creativity, enthusiasm, and excitement with us. Being mothers, we are continually involved with our children's schools, expanding art awareness through our volunteer efforts. We have a strong sense of what children like to do artistically, while combining fun and learning at the same time. We strive to establish a positive and stimulating environment in which youth can grow while attaining an appreciation of the world of art.

We strongly believe that our combined talents would benefit Wellington Art League's Summer Program immensely. Blending our expertise to develop, coordinate, and lead your programming is our "forte." We look forward to meeting with you in the near future to learn more about the positions and to exchange ideas.

Thank you for your time and consideration, Ms. Hudson.

Sincerely,

Sally Mitchell Klein   Helen Mitchell Young

Sally Mitchell Klein
7181 North Cooper Street
San Francisco, CA 94112
(101) 555-3453

Helen Mitchell Young
3812 Crescent Drive
San Francisco, CA 94112
(101) 555-2445

Target   Fine Art Day Camp Director and Fine Art Day Camp Assistant Director for the Wellington Art League

Relevant Creative Abilities   Established a creative design painting company, Incredible Art!, which has produced a variety of projects in commercial and residential facilities throughout California.
Featured in St. Mary's Guild Decorator Showhouse and Johnson's Place Restaurant. Work has incorporated a melange of surfaces, including fabric, canvas, furniture, and walls. Have been given liberties by clients to create unique and personalized designs and have consistently achieved customer satisfaction on all projects.

As Team Arts Co-Chairmen of Blaker Mill School, developed, initiated, and directed successful programs that expanded student awareness of and involvement in the arts beyond the school curriculum. They consisted of:

- smART Week—Created and directed a weeklong art fair that focused on activities involving the enjoyment of the fine arts and included the entire student body.
- Creative-Facts—Established a monthly fine arts newsletter directed toward students, staff, and families.
- Created a student gallery; oversaw a fund-raiser that showcased fine arts student art in a stationary exhibit; and formed a school Fine Arts Committee.
- Instructors in Blaker Mill's After-School Activities programs, individually specializing in cartooning and comic strips, painting, and drawing. Taught students to create and produce projects with paper, canvas, fabric, and an assortment of materials.
- Oversaw "Living Works," a permanent collective painting art collection involving an artist and 600 students working individually and collaboratively.
- Expanded student and parent involvement through Visiting Artists fund-raising programs.

Education   B.S./Painting Emphasis, 1987, and Interior Design, 1997–1999
INDIANA UNIVERSITY, Bloomington, Indiana
- Helen has taken multiple continuing education classes at the San Francisco Art League and the San Francisco Museum of Art, and a painting and drawing course at Oxbow, the school of the Art Institute of Chicago, in Saugatuck, Michigan.
- Jointly authored "Celebrate the Earth," *San Fran's Child,* 4/99.

Marilyn Taylor
1534 Sheridan Avenue
Los Angeles, CA 83110
(410) 555-4554
mtaylor@email.com

Summary of Qualifications

Diversified background in international travel and hospitality with extensive experience in multilingual, multicultural environments. Proven ability to transcend cultural and language differences and bridge those diversities in creating strong customer and employee relationships. Detail-oriented, hands-on professional with excellent organizational and problem-solving abilities.

Relevant Experience

ORGANIZATIONAL MANAGEMENT:
- *Staff development, training, and supervision in airline and hospitality industries: Developed multicultural and multilingual curriculums, including training procedures on Western management styles, philosophy, and culture for over 700 employees of a major Chinese hotel.*
- *Demonstrate leadership and interpersonal skills by managing staff through influence, positive motivation, and example, creating a team effort that results in superior customer service.*
- *Efficient coordination of services, interacting effectively between operations, customer service, public relations, and support staffs.*

PUBLIC RELATIONS:
- *Provided individualized client service, encompassing needs assessment, crisis intervention, and problem resolution for people from diverse backgrounds.*
- *Public relations representative, media liaison, and interpreter at major international trade shows for high-profile multinational corporations.*

CONVENTION AND MEETING PLANNING:
- *Acquired knowledge of convention and meeting planning, with a solid foundation in hospitality relations, contract/vendor negotiations, F & B, travel and tourism, entertainment management, and audiovisual conferencing.*

Work History

1997–Present   **Interpreter, Project Coordinator, Media Liaison**
NOWEA International Convention and Trade Show Center, Munich, Germany

1995–1997   **Training Manager**
Beijing Green Lake Hotel, Beijing, China

1980–1995   **Purser/Flight Attendant**
Trans World Airlines, New York

Education

Conference and Meeting Management, *New York University, 1998*
English, Cambridge University, *Cambridge, England, UK*
Advanced French Studies, *Alliance Francaise, Besancon, France*
Spanish-Language Studies, *Berlitz School, Palma de Mallorca, Spain*
Liberal Arts Degree, *Schwestern U. L. Frau, Mulhausen, Germany*

Languages

Fluent in German, English, French, and Spanish

Cynthia Snyder

8323 Harrison Way ◆ Snellville, Georgia 30278 ◆ (404) 555-3939

Summary of Qualifications

Comprehensive experience in office administration with significant focus on compiling data relevant to educational programs, editing and distributing educational materials, and coordinating seminars and training sessions for educators. Record of consistent achievement; dependable and trustworthy. Ability to handle multiple responsibilities, set priorities, communicate ideas to others, and respond positively to demanding situations. Computer-literate and detail-oriented.

Experience

CIVIL AIR PATROL—USAF
Newport Air Force Base, Georgia   1981 to 2000

Administrative Support Assistant to the Director of Educational Programs, 1997 to 2000
- Edited and proofread aerospace textbooks, instructor guides, and workbooks used in colleges and universities. Verified grammar, spelling, punctuation, and capitalization; assessed contents for clear expression, accuracy, and appropriate paragraph formation.
- Composed and processed manuscripts, lists, and business communications using various computer applications.
- Organized and compiled data that facilitated productive and beneficial educational workshops.
- Acted as liaison between educational organizations and military personnel.

Secretary for the Deputy of Staff, Aerospace Education and Cadet Program, 1981 to 1997
- Served as Director of Information (1987 through 1997) for the annual National Congress on Aviation and Space Education; convention was attended by approximately 1,200 educators, principals, and administrators (cosponsored by the Civil Air Patrol, NASA, and the FAA).
- Established procedures and controls pertaining to registration, recording of financial data, and the material preparation/distribution for the Aerospace Education Leadership Course.
- Maintained inventory and directed distribution of promotional and educational materials to instructors throughout the United States.
- Assisted with preparation and administration of budgets; processed purchase orders.

DEPUTY CHIEF OF STAFF/INTELLIGENCE
Bradford Air Force Base, Georgia   1967 to 1980

- Performed multiple tasks relating to handling classified material within the Air Force Special Security Office vault, which required Top-Secret Clearance.

Intelligence Clerk for Directorate of Intelligence, *1980 to 1981*
Intelligence Clerk for Evaluations and Applications Division, *1973 to 1980*
Clerk Stenographer, Analysis Division, *1970 to 1973*
Clerk Stenographer, Activities Division, *1969 to 1970*
Clerk Stenographer for Deputy Chief of Staff Intelligence, *1967 to 1968*

Education

PERRY BUSINESS SCHOOL, Brunswick, Georgia
Certificate of Completion, Business/Secretarial Course

Patricia Eller

6867 Walnut Bend Road
Westminster, CO 80030
(303) 555-1060
pateller@email.com

Goal and Profit–Oriented Marketing Director

Marketing and Promotion:

- Increased census at 40 facilities in 5 states through problem-solving with facility staff to overcome marketing obstacles.
- Created and wrote marketing materials (brochures, direct-mail pieces, advertisements, and newsletters) for 200 facilities.
- Implemented new product development, including market research, financial analysis, design of product, manufacturing, and distribution.
- Developed and organized a public relations plan for 250,000 potential clients.
- Coordinated hundreds of special events, attracting up to 6,000 new customers to one event.
- Improved guest relations in over 50 facilities in 7 states through training and coauthored plan.
- Strengthened profitability through the execution of semiannual marketing plans, including upgraded suites, rehabilitation programs, and specialized care units.

Sales:

- Record-setting census increase of 55% in 12 weeks through internal and external promotional programs.
- Tripled Medicare census in 23 nursing homes in 4 states.
- Multiplied sales calls by 120% through training and motivation of administrative staff from 23 facilities.
- Developed and trained over 350 employees in marketing, public speaking, guest relations, and sales information.
- Motivated and trained sales team of 16, increasing sales by $150,000 in 1 month.

Supervision and Organization:

- Analytical and evaluation proficiency resulting from start-up procedures for this company.
- Allocated and managed $250K budget for grand-opening event.
- Recruited, hired, supervised, and evaluated 16 employees.
- Conducted performance analyses consisting of obstacle identification, negotiation, resolution, and implementation.

Experience:

Owner/CEO, Creative Results, Marketing & Promotions Firm	1990–Present
Owner/Manager, Grandmommy's Cottage, Ltd. (Retail Shop)	1990–1993
Director of Marketing and Sales, Charter Hospital of Ft. Collins	1989–1990
Regional Marketing Consultant, Hillhaven Corporation	1987–1989
Regional Marketing Director, ARA Living Centers	1981–1987

Education:

Graduate Certificate, University of Northern Colorado	1982
M.S., Pennsylvania State University	1980
B.S., York College of Pennsylvania	1977

TODD RICHARDSON

PERMANENT ADDRESS:
834 Bromley Place, East Brunswick, NJ 08816
(908) 555-3743

UNIVERSITY ADDRESS:
2101 Spaulding Street, Amherst, MA 01002
(413) 555-9382

"I have rarely, in my ten years in the hospitality industry, encountered an individual, in the dawn of his career, who has shown as much promise as Todd Richardson." ***

HIGHLIGHTS
- Expect to graduate in June 2000 from well-respected HRTA program
- Proven self-starter who does what needs to be done without being asked
- Team player with track record of establishing productive work relationships
- Friendly, outgoing, excellent customer-relations abilities
- **Computer skills:** Windows 98, Microsoft Office 2000, WordPerfect, Lotus 1-2-3, Q&A, Delphi space-management software

EDUCATION

University of Massachusetts, Amherst, MA
B.A., Hotel, Restaurant, and Travel Administration (expected June 2000)
Area of Concentration: Food Service Management

HOSPITALITY EXPERIENCE

Scanticon-Princeton Conference Center Hotel, Princeton, NJ
Intern (Summer 1999)
- Worked for Conference Services (7 weeks) and Food and Beverage Department (5 weeks).
- Received a highly complimentary, unsolicited letter of recommendation from the Director of Conference Services specifically praising my initiative and interpersonal skills.***
- *Conference Services:* Responsible for preparation of meeting rooms, audiovisual equipment, internal accounting documents, distribution of reports concerning incoming conference groups, and coordination with group representatives.
- *Food and Beverage Department:* Management of dining room, including hospitality, guest check reconciliation, preparation of floor plans, beverage control, and direct supervision of wait staff.

Pizza Hut, North Brunswick, NJ
Cook (Summer 1998)
- Responsible for daily setup of kitchen before opening and food preparation for lunch. Waited and bussed tables. Operated computerized cash register and serviced credit card receipts.

VOLUNTEER ACTIVITIES

Phi Delta Theta Fraternity, Amherst, MA
Caterer (Fall 1997, 1998, and 1999)
- Sole responsibility for planning, purchasing, cooking, and serving food for the fraternity's Alumni Weekend (twice) and Parents' Weekend (twice). Average attendance was 125 people.
Made all burgers, salads, etc. from scratch.

Phi Delta Theta Fraternity, Amherst, MA
Kitchen Steward (January to December 1997)
- Established kitchen procedures, many still in use, for newly chartered chapter of this fraternity.
- Responsible for food budget, purchasing food supplies, interviewing and hiring kitchen personnel, supervising kitchen and dining room operation, and preparing food.

OTHER EXPERIENCE

First Aid Unit, University of Massachusetts, Amherst, MA
EMT/CPR Coordinator (1998 to Present)
- Responsible for first aid at all university athletic events, concerts, and Fine Arts Center activities.
- Coordinated and instructed CPR program sponsored by the University's Environmental Health and Safety Office.

SPECIAL ACHIEVEMENTS
- Certificate in basic mixology
- Emergency Medical Technician, New Jersey and Massachusetts
- American Red Cross CPR and First Aid Instructor
- Chosen to participate in "Career Shadowing" program by the University of Massachusetts Alumni Association of New York
- Certified Water Safety Instructor

SUE BLACKARD
10345 NW SECOND COURT
MIAMI, FL 33150
(305) 555-5637
Pager: (305) 555-1234
sublack428@mailme.com

November 3, 2000

Roosevelt Services, Inc.
8643 North Market Street
Miami, FL 33152

Dear Ms. Roosevelt,

In the interest of exploring employment opportunities with your organization, enclosed is my resume, which profiles my background and professional experience.

My substantial hands-on experience consists equally of in-depth knowledge and ability in both state-of-the-art computer technology to support multimillion-dollar production programs and intangible sales for a major New York Stock Exchange communications company.

Each position I've held has required graphic design and layout, extreme attention to text and accounting files, as well as strict adherence to various deadlines. I have also needed the flexibility to adapt to many different management and compensation programs, with many hours of on-the-spot overtime. In addition, I've answered or returned up to 80 calls in a day and have demonstrated patience and tact in resolving client and staff problems. On a freelance basis I produce desktop publishing and typesetting for private clients.

If you are seeking a well-qualified and productive individual who has been involved in multidisciplinary operations within highly competitive markets—someone equally at home with computers and sales—I believe I am a viable candidate for the position. I would appreciate a personal interview to discuss the ways in which my areas of expertise can bring immediate results and assist you in accomplishing your goals.

I look forward to meeting with you.

Sincerely,

Sue Blackard

Sue Blackard

Enclosure

Excellent Applicant Definitely Interview

SUE BLACKARD

10345 NW Second Court
Miami, FL 33150
(305) 555-5637

Employment Highlights

SALES
- Top-producing sales professional; consistently successful in increasing revenues, capturing key accounts, and winning major market share.
- Among the top three salespeople of 30 representatives selling real estate advertising.
- Consistently exceeded weekly and monthly quotas.
- Extremely adaptable to changing situations and job requirements.

DATA PROCESSING
- **Software:** WordPerfect 9... Microsoft Office 2000... Q&A database... Crosstalk... Mastertracks PC... MusicPrinter Plus... Microsoft Publisher... Windows and Mac OS environments...
- **Hardware:** IBM-compatible PC... Atex Systems... various *Miami Herald* data-entry and accounting systems... iMac
- MIDI-based computer network to write, record, and publish music... digital and analog formats...
- Software installation... Hardware troubleshooting

Employment History

HALLMARK PRESS, Miami, FL   9/98–Present
Assistant Production Manager
  Coordinate job programming and oversee quality control from preproduction to bindery... Order materials and expedite vendor services to meet production schedules and deadlines... Analyze, troubleshoot, and resolve client problems... Supervise staff of three...

MOIRA JAYE REALTY, Aventura, FL   4/96–9/98
Office Manager/Assistant Leasing Agent
  Oversaw all commercial leasing office operations... Showed the property to prospective tenants and negotiated leases... On-site liaison between tenants and management... Liaison between clients and architects, designers, contractors
- Upgraded overall computer operations; installed Q&A database to track prospective clients; implemented Microsoft Office 97; implemented commission-tracking procedures...

THE MIAMI HERALD, Miami, FL   1/86–3/96
Classified Account Representative
  Sold, serviced, and developed up to 150 advertising accounts, representing approximately $1.5 million in annual revenue... Consistent record of increasing responsibilities and accomplishments:
- Initiated hands-on training of newly promoted Account Representatives in 1994.
- Sold and serviced two account bases in 1993, increasing revenue of both by 30%.
- Increased "Florida New Homes Directory" coverage from one to four times weekly, boosting annual revenue from $600,000 to $1.2 million, 1992.
- Acted as "user liaison" to develop in-house classified ad data-entry system; provided extensive input into the Classified Training Manual, currently in use by the company, 1991.
- Became responsible for sales, service, billing, layout, and design of "The Florida Home Directory," 1990.
- Promoted to Dade Contract Sales (real estate accounts), 1989; promoted to Broward Contract Sales and Telemarketing Sales, 1987.

Education

Miami-Dade Community College, Miami, FL
Studied Music, 1985

Stephanie Devine

2233 Meadow Lane
Scotch Plains, New Jersey 07076
(312) 555-1234
Pager: (312) 555-4231

Professional Registered Nurse with extensive experience developing Utilization Review Programs. Proven ability to ensure quality health care while containing costs within the hospital environment. Skilled in coordinating programs and interfacing with professional medical and administrative staff.

CAREER EXPERIENCE:

Mayer Institute for Rehabilitation, Middletown, New Jersey   6/95–Present
Coordinator of Professional Standards
- ▲ Developed start-up Utilization Review Program for this 240-bed hospital with three sites. Prepared Utilization Review plan as per Medicare guidelines and implemented in six months' time.
- ▲ Created an in-service training program for medical, social service, and administrative staff to facilitate compliance with Medicare standards. Continue to address staff training needs with programs including creation of an orientation manual and special material for new hires.

Boger County Jail, Hoboken, New Jersey   1/94–6/95
Correctional Nurse (part time)
- ▲ Provided a wide range of nursing services for 1,100 inmates, including emergency medical treatment, psychiatric intervention, and childbirth. Successfully performed well under pressure as sole medical professional in often-tense situations.

Meridian Peer Review Organization, Hoboken, New Jersey   1/94–6/95
Review Coordinator
- ▲ Performed concurrent/retrospective reviews of medical records for major hospitals in Hudson, Bergen, and Essex counties. Verified that medical necessity and quality of care adhered to Medicare/ Medicaid guidelines.
- ▲ Coordinated the start-up of the Ambulatory Care Review Program. Developed review procedures and performed first reviews of this type in state. Ascertained the lack of cost-effective results for further continuation.

Roosevelt General Medical Center, Trenton, New Jersey   11/86–1/94
Staff/Charge Nurse
- ▲ Managed several units, including Medical-Surgical, Coronary Care, and Emergency Room.
- ▲ Supervised up to 45 patients and a staff of three nurses and paraprofessionals.

CERTIFICATIONS/AFFILIATIONS:

New Jersey Registered Nurse License; CPR-certified
Member of State and National Association for Healthcare Quality
- ▲ Delegate to National Convention for three years.
- ▲ Served on Legislative Committee for State Association.

EDUCATION:

Roosevelt General Medical Center School of Nursing, Trenton, New Jersey
Diploma in Nursing with Associate in Science conferred by County College, Cranford, New Jersey
Kean College, Union, New Jersey, Matriculated in B.S. Degree Program/Psychology Major
- ▲ Selected for *Who's Who Among Students in American Junior Colleges.*

DEAN DUNAGAN
6677 Kenwood Drive
Wolcott, CT 28210
(704) 555-1122

SUMMARY OF QUALIFICATIONS

- *Over twenty years of comprehensive experience in tending and managing cocktail bars. Four years of schooling in mixology. Thrive in a fast-paced, demanding environment.*

- *Self-directed, organized professional with high standards of conduct for patrons and a willingness to enforce limits. Excellent interpersonal and public relations skills.*

- *Managerial skills include inventory control, personnel supervision, and customer management.*

- *Superior memory and attention to detail. Exceptional recall of drink recipes (without reference to manuals or notes) and patrons' preferred drinks.*

PROFESSIONAL EXPERIENCE

Veterans of Foreign Wars, *Wolcott, CT*   *1997–Present*
Bar Manager/Bartender

- *Open and close business; handle all cash transactions. Stock bar. Supervise employees; manage patrons.*

- *Suggested and implemented periodic drink specials; increased daily patronage and raised profits by 20%.*

- *Originate exotic drinks. Expanded inventory of stock to promote business with exotic mixes.*

- *Recognized by supervisor as "best bartender that ever worked here."*

American Legion, *Plainville, CT*   *1975–1997*
Bartender (Part-time)

M.H. Rhodes, *Avon, CT*   *1976–1996*
Supervisor

Oversaw the work of 20 employees on assembly line, fabricating timing devices.

EDUCATION

Hartfield School of Mixology, *Hartford, CT*
Graduated

Farmtown High School, *Farmington, CT*
Graduated

AFFILIATIONS

American Legion Auxiliary
Chaplain (9 years)
Jr. Vice President (1 year)

Katherine M. Peale

5814 Petersburg Parkway
Chicago, IL 30035
(708) 555-1223
kmpeale@email.com

—SUMMARY OF QUALIFICATIONS—

An accomplished Associate Buyer with proven ability to increase profitability
through product and private-label development.

—EXPERIENCE—

J.C. PENNEY, Chicago, IL   1995–Present

Associate Buyer—Career Tops/Bottoms
Assistant Buyer—Career Tops/Bottoms
Merchandising Department Assistant
Intern—Assistant to Buyer—Sportswear and Dresses

✔ Responsible for developing a complete private-label program.
✔ Work closely with domestic and overseas manufacturers, designers,
merchandise managers, and fabric and trim resources.
✔ Research and develop new resources.
✔ Negotiate price and delivery terms with vendors.
✔ Attend national and local trade shows to remain up-to-date on current and emerging fashion trends.
✔ Visit factories to monitor quality.
✔ Approve lab dips.
✔ Monitor store sales, requests, and inventory to maximize sales efforts.
✔ Analyze and project sales by line, style, and color to identify high-volume products.
✔ Perform gross margin analysis and forecasting.
✔ Provide product information to stores.
✔ Determine pricing of missy and petite categories.
✔ Participate in pricing and markdown strategies.

Accomplishments:
Currently exceeding sales plan for career bottoms by 34%, representing an 88% gain over 1996.
Increased blouse sales by 130% and revenues by 163%, 1996 versus 1995.

HENRI BENDEL, New York, NY   1994–1995

Stylist, Intimate Apparel
✔ Responsible for personal client book.
✔ Assisted with display set-ups, merchandising, inventory, and cashiering.

—EDUCATION—

The Paris Fashion Institute, Paris, France   12/95–2/96
✔ Participated in numerous seminars given by fashion industry leaders.
✔ Toured couture houses and took part in merchandising workshops geared to
to enhancing my knowledge of the European market.

Fashion Institute of Technology, New York, NY   1995
B.S., Marketing, Merchandise Management, Magna Cum Laude
A.A.S., Fashion Buying and Merchandising, Magna Cum Laude

Honors:
Dean's List and National Dean's List
National Academic Honor Society

Laura B. Towne

Career History

Reynolds Enterprises, Chester, Maine

Retail drug chain with 86 locations in three states employing 1,800. Annual sales volume: $167 million.

Assistant Vice President/Controller
1994–2000

Assistant Vice President/Finance
1993–94

Assistant Vice President/Consumer Receivables *1990–93*

Credit Manager
1988–90

Assistant Credit Manager/Collection Manager *1986–88*

Accounting and Credit Clerk
1983–86

Manage day-to-day operations of accounting department, including payroll, accounts payable, sales/cash reports, and general ledger.

Hire, train, evaluate, and supervise 18–22 employees.

Calculate inventories on a LIFO basis and perform other year-end analyses including cost capitalization.

Conduct internal auditing, account analysis, and government, bank, and internal reporting.

Participate in selecting banks and benefit plan administrators and submitting recommendations to top management.

Profile

Financial Management Professional with 17-year record of service and promotion for retail drug chain.

Team-oriented manager who works harmoniously with coworkers and top-level management to achieve company goals.

Implemented numerous cost-control programs, including conversion from manual methods of accounting and tracking to computerized systems.

Proficient in coordinating and controlling the process of auditing, analyzing, reporting, and making recommendations to improve overall management of company's financial and human resources.

Education

Harper College
Wheat Fields, Maine
M.B.A. (Magna Cum Laude), 1993

B.S. Accounting (Magna Cum Laude, Alpha Chi National Honor Society), 1986

Address

97 Lakeville Drive
Seaport, Maine 04222

(207) 555-8151
laurab@email.com

JEFFREY S. CRAWFORD, ESQ.

654 Birch Avenue, Auburn, MA 01501
(508) 555-9887

EDUCATION

WESTERN NEW ENGLAND SCHOOL OF LAW, Springfield, MA
- Awarded an academic scholarship. Graduated Cum Laude, 1992.
- Received the Am Jur Award in Business Organization and Trial Methods.
- Member of the Law Review.

CLARK UNIVERSITY, Worcester, MA
- B.A., Government, 1984. Awarded an academic scholarship.

PUBLICATIONS

"Labor Law—The St. Francis II Disparity of Interests Test—Is It Necessary?"
9 W.N.E.L. Rev. 2 (1992)

EXPERIENCE

1998 to Present

DEPARTMENT OF MENTAL HEALTH, Providence, RI
Program Manager Specialist IV
- Work with senior managers of the department to design a system of public managed care to serve the mentally ill throughout the state.
- Negotiate and draft reimbursement contracts with private-sector acute-care hospitals.
- Analyze, evaluate, and advise department leadership regarding proposed and pending legislation. Assist in drafting legislation and regulations promulgated by the department.
- Acted as Counsel to the Commissioner during seven-month House Post-Audit Bureau in investigation of the department's privatization initiative.

1995 to 1998

PRIVATE PRACTICE, Worcester, MA
- Extensive work in all aspects of health-care law. Clients include insurers, HMOs, physicians, and dentists.
- General Counsel to Insurance Cost Control, Inc., an employee benefits consulting firm specializing in public-sector clients.
- General practice included closely held corporations, partnerships, and sole proprietors.

1995

HEALTH COST CONTROL, INC., Worcester, MA
General Counsel—Vice President for Large Accounts
- Designed the legal framework for self-funded managed-care networks, developed self-funded employee health benefit plans, and drafted group health benefit contracts.
- Represented the company in numerous negotiations with hospitals, HMOs, PPOs, insurers, and reinsurers. Also appeared before state regulatory boards.
- Participated in a variety of operational functions, including transactional work, negotiating software licensing agreements, negotiating real estate leases, and employee relations law.

1992 to 1994

DEWEY & CHEATEM, PC, Worcester, MA
Associate—Corporate Law Dept., Health Law Practice Area
- Advised HMOs on operating issues, and hospitals and nursing homes on operating and patient-care issues.
- Extensive work with the Division of Insurance and other state regulators.
- Represented individual physicians before the Board of Registration.
- Prepared a wide variety of contracts for hospitals and HMOs, including subscriber plan agreements.
- Corporate law practice included organizing corporations, stock transfers, and preparation of finance documents; drafted partnership agreements and joint-venture agreements.

AFFILIATIONS

- *Member,* American Bar Association
- *Member,* Massachusetts Bar Association
- *Member,* National Health Lawyers Association
- *Fellow,* American Academy of Hospital Attorneys

DOUGLAS RODGERS

1122 First Drive North
Northampton, MA 01061
(413) 555-2233

SUMMARY:

A decade of experience in senior management, with expertise in general management, manufacturing, marketing, materials, international operations, and budgeting/finance. Stable and promotable, with over 25 years at the same company. Willing to accept the right middle-management position with growth potential.

ACCOMPLISHMENTS:

Vice President/General Manager, STC Services, Inc., Boston, MA

Growth and Diversification

- Expanded Canadian distribution system to annual sales of approximately $2 million.
- Organized and participated in acquisitions screening team, resulting in purchase of $1.5 million product line.
- Adapted product line marketing to rapidly changing technologies; successfully repositioned product mix toward new markets and distribution channels, resulting in $3 million in new annual sales.
- Used existing manufacturing process to develop new product line, generating over $1 million in new annual sales.
- Developed new distribution channel for private-label OEM products, with new sales of $85 million annually.
- Negotiated government contract, yielding $2 million in annual sales.
- Redesigned existing product to better meet customer needs, yielding immediate 10% increase in sales.
- Achieved 15% increase in profits in first year as General Manager.

Efficiency/Cost Control:

- Reduced inventory by $1 million while maintaining full level of service.
- Relocated an acquisition from Florida to Massachusetts, reducing floor space by 50% with no interruption in customer service.
- Moved several processes in-house, resulting in dramatic cost savings and efficiency increases:
  - Began manufacturing previously imported product line (50% savings).
  - Developed in-house technology to produce previously purchased raw materials (35% savings).
  - Replaced service bureau with in-house data processing; developed order-entry system that improved turnaround by two days.
- Redesigned computer-aided manufacturing templates to reduce waste and decrease material costs by 35%.

General Management:

- Full profit and loss responsibility.
- Reduced average days outstanding for receivables by instituting tighter controls.
- Improved employee morale by instituting regular meetings and increasing possibilities for communication.

WORK HISTORY:

STC Services, Inc., Boston, MA, 1973–Present
- Vice President/General Manager, 1995–1998
- Group Vice President/Operations, 1994–1995
- General Manager/Operations, 1991–1994
- Vice President/Operations, 1989–1991
- Originally hired as production control manager, 1973; several promotions with increasing responsibility, 1973–1989

MBI Corporation, Inc., Stoughton, MA, 1971–1972
- Manufacturing Manager

MOLLIE A. EVANSTON, L.P.C.
1641 Westridge
Portage, Michigan 49002
(616) 555-9876

CREDENTIALS

- School Counselor Endorsement, 1999
- Licensed Professional Counselor, 1999
- Community Health Services Specialty Certification, Alcohol and Drug Abuse, 1999
- Elementary Continuing Certificate, 1989

EDUCATION

Western Michigan University, *Kalamazoo, Michigan*

- M.A., Counselor Education and Counseling Psychology, December 1998
- B.S., Elementary Education, 1983

PROFESSIONAL EXPERIENCE

On-Site Practicum, *Western Michigan University, Kalamazoo, MI, Winter 1998*

- Counseled adult clients in personal, social, emotional, and career-development issues with continuous supervision provided by a licensed psychologist.

Field Practicum, *Kalamazoo Public Schools, Kalamazoo, MI, Fall 1998*

- Developed orientation program for new elementary students in two buildings.
- Observed and conducted interviews with individuals and groups of students, grades K–12.
- Planned and presented self-esteem–building lessons for kindergarten and first-grade students.
- Assisted with the administration of Differential Aptitude Tests to eighth-grade students.
- Observed and assisted in sexual harassment unit presented to ninth-grade students.

Elementary Teacher, *Jones Elementary School, Detroit, MI, 1989–1995*

- Provided instruction to classroom of fourth-grade students in all subject areas.
- Coordinated fund-raising activities for various class projects and field trips.
- Wrote and implemented Symatic Integrated unit on the human body.
- Developed and used effective activities to encourage individual self-esteem.

Compensatory Aide Coordinator, *Delton Elementary School, Delton, MI, 1988–1989*

- Instructed grades 1–8 in remedial reading and math skills.
- Administered various achievement and assessment tests to students.

Article III Math Instructor, *Delton Elementary School, Delton, MI, 1984–1988*

- Provided specialized materials in conjunction with class work to meet individual needs.
- Developed goal objectives in coordination with standard math requirements.
- Conferred with teachers, parents, and administrators regarding individual progress.
- Served as yearbook staff director and editor.

> One hundred years from now it will not matter what my bank account was, the sort of house I lived in, or the kind of car I drove but the world may be different because I was important in the life of a child.
>
> —Anonymous

PHILIP L. HUNTER, JR.

2340 Palaco Grande, Naples, FL 33905 ▪ (813) 555-3351

OBJECTIVE

A position in Financial Services that uses my skills in planning, research, marketing, and business development.

QUALIFICATIONS SUMMARY

- 19 years of financial management
- Strategic planning
- Portfolio management
- Lending and collections
- Human resources management
- Policy development

- Marketing and advertising
- Market research
- Business development
- MIS and data-processing management
- Financial analysis
- Board relations

ACHIEVEMENTS

- Instituted marketing, advertising, and sales functions.
- Developed yearly marketing plan and budget, balancing costs, quality, and effectiveness.
- Increased assets from $16 million to $70 million.
- Supervised a staff of 40.
- Managed revenues of $6.5 million.
- Built and opened corporate office and branch locations.
- Established a full-service product line and relationship-based culture.
- Instituted strategic planning and management by objectives.
- Reorganized trade association and central bank.
- Upgraded data-processing and information systems.
- Merged or acquired numerous employee groups.
- Developed and marketed a new name and image for the institution.
- Installed a commissioned sales and tracking program including testing, training manuals, and a sales award program.
- Designed marketing campaigns using direct mail, display advertising, telemarketing, and calling programs.
- Installed the first shared ATM network in the state.
- Added commissioned originators to generate mortgage loans with Realtors and contractors.
- Produced various market studies—focus group, demographic, branch expansion, employee attitude, and customer service.
- Served on various national and local marketing committees.

EXPERIENCE

COASTAL CREDIT UNION, Naples, FL
1981–2000 Vice President, Executive Vice President, President, and Chief Executive Officer

EDUCATION

B.B.A. University of Miami, Miami, FL 1981

BUSINESS AND CIVIC ACTIVITIES

- Member, Federal Legislative/Regulatory Committee (CUNA)
- Member, American Management Association—President's Association

Susan L. Miller

8347 South 186 West
Salt Lake City, Utah 84105
(801) 555-9238
susanlmiller@email.com

Qualifications

- ◆ Recent Interior Design graduate, with both residential and commercial experience.
- ◆ Strengths include product knowledge and application, space planning, color and texture specifications, creation of presentation materials, accessorizing expertise, and a passion for interior design.
- ◆ Proficient in theoretical design.
- ◆ AutoCAD training and experience.
- ◆ In-depth knowledge of furniture design history—styles, themes, and origination.
- ◆ Possess good taste and a natural design ability.
- ◆ Articulate and professional, qualified for client interaction.

Experience

Interior Design Specialist   2000
Michael's Furnishings and Gifts   Salt Lake City, Utah
Provided on-site design services as well as private residential interior design consultation. Initiated, conducted, and completed interior design engagements. Assisted in display merchandising for in-store furnishings.

Internship in Interior Design   2000
Medical Center of Utah   Salt Lake City, Utah
Provided space planning for neurology wing. Selection of colors, finishes, and treatments for other projects.

Clinical Research Manager   1997–1999
National Semiconductor   Salt Lake City, Utah
Liaison for third-phase pharmaceutical research studies, coordinating with personnel, clinical research organizations, and study sponsors. Maintained source documents and records, and completed case report forms.

Receptionist   1997
Diversified Business Services   Salt Lake City, Utah
Research, telephone, and office administration responsibilities.

Work-Exchange Program   1996
Merchandising Representative   Paris, France
In-store product sales and demonstrations.

Education

1999–2000   Associate of Applied Science in Interior Design
                         Weber State University, Ogden, Utah

1992–1996   Bachelor of Arts in Psychology
                         Weber College, Grand Rapids, Iowa

1994   "Study in Spain" intensive language course
                         Denia, Spain

BRIAN ASHMORE
962 East 12th Street
New York, New York 11210
(718) 555-0588
bashmore@mojo.net

QUALIFICATIONS: Increasing responsibilities in areas including

- ▶ Budgeting
- ▶ Contract Negotiations
- ▶ Policies
- ▶ Computers

- ▶ Variance
- ▶ Planning and Analysis
- ▶ General Ledger Maintenance
- ▶ Supervisory Management

PROFILE: Currently serve as a Budget Analyst for R.H. Macy's & Co… formerly held positions in the buying and retail-management areas of the corporation… consistently promoted to increasing financial-based responsibilities and projects… known as a results-oriented manager with excellent analytical and forecasting abilities…use a team approach to effectively reduce costs and increase the bottom line.

EDUCATION: **Boston College, Carroll School of Management**
Bachelor of Science, May 1996
Major: Marketing
Concentration: Human Resources Management

EXPERIENCE:
1999–Present

R.H. MACY'S & CO., New York, NY
Budget Analyst
Plan and analyze all aspects of the direct mail, broadcast media, and administrative advertising budgets on a seasonal basis. Responsible for the successful closing of accounts on a monthly basis. Work closely with creative directors to reduce costs and adhere to seasonal plans.

Responsibilities include preparing budget variance reports, creating and analyzing spreadsheets, processing invoices for payments, negotiating prices on contractual agreements, and working with the President of Advertising to determine the most efficient system upgrades to reduce costs.

- Reduced budget by 12% while increasing payment of accounts receivable by 5%.
- Instituted new company procedures for employee compensation and settlement packages.
- Created a tax law guideline to be used during vendor negotiations.
- Responsible for planning, purchasing, and distributing the "Purchase with Purchase" programs for R.H. Macy's national program events.
- Possess computer skills in databases and application systems that include Novell Netware, Paradox, Excel, Lotus 1-2-3, Quattro Pro, Microsoft Word, and Sabre.

1998–1999

R.H. MACY'S & CO., New York, NY
Assistant Buyer for Jones New York
Responsible for the operations of a $30 million better sportswear business. Planned buying operations with the administrator of Liz Claiborne and Jones New York, which totaled $110 million in gross sales. Analyzed sales, stock levels, and stock turn to project future business strategies.

1997–1998

MACY'S KING'S PLAZA, Brooklyn, NY
Sales Manager, Men's Sport Furnishings
Responsible for the supervision of 41 sales associates. Increased sales volume 2.5% to 4.2 million annually, the third largest volume in Macy's East 59-store chain.
Implemented policies to increase customer service and sales; spread the company in sportswear by 5.3%.

STEVE GEORGE

1234 Event Street • San Diego, CA 12345
(619) 555-4567
sgeorge@email.com

OBJECTIVE: Position as an Electronics Engineering Technician.

SUMMARY: Over eight years of experience in electronics, including design, modification, and technical support of SATCOM, computer hardware/software, communication, radar, and navigation systems. An exceptional technician consistently recognized for engineering money-saving solutions to complex technical problems.

PROFESSIONAL EXPERIENCE:

Engineering Technician   12/98–Present
Naval Center for Tactical Systems Interoperability   San Diego, CA

Provided technical support for a tactical data-link communications system involving bit-oriented transmission of digital information. Assisted in developing interface design standards and system certification. Provided system hardware and software consultation, research, development, and modification for U.S. and allied forces.

- Researched, configured, and installed newest data information link, saving over $20,000 in outside contract funds.
- Established and directed a remote test site for data-link system testing on allied ships. Saved thousands in operational expenses associated with fleet travel to continental U.S. test site.

Senior Maintenance Technician/Shop Supervisor   11/96–12/98
Shore Intermediate Maintenance Activity   Long Beach, CA

Supervised the work of 26 electronics technicians in the maintenance and repair of radio and satellite communication systems, electronic navigation equipment, and air/surface search radar systems. Directed calibration/repair of general and special-purpose test equipment. Coordinated production, including scheduling, job assignments, and acquisition of tools, equipment, and materials. Conducted quality-control inspections and evaluated employee performance verbally and in writing.

- Instituted an in-shop test equipment repair program, eliminating the need to contract out repairs. Saved over $100,000 and was awarded the Navy Achievement Medal.
- Installed a remote test bed to test digital interrogation systems in a neutral environment and to facilitate technician refresher training. Enabled more rapid fault isolation and increased employee technical proficiency.

Maintenance Technician   2/93–11/96
USS *Ogden*   Long Beach, CA

Maintained and repaired air/surface search radar, and provided technical support and consultation on a wide range of electronics systems.

- Affected manufacturer-level repairs on complex gun-mount elevation circuitry, saving thousands in outside repair costs.
- Adapted Marine Corps global positioning satellite navigation system for use aboard nine U.S. ships during Operation Desert Storm. Reconfigured wiring, cabling, and power source. Enabled ships to pinpoint their global positions to within 25 feet.

EDUCATION AND TECHNICAL TRAINING:

Undergraduate Electronics, Chapman University, San Diego, CA. Enrolled Fall 1999.
Electronics Engineering Technology, Los Angeles Harbor College, Wilmington, CA, 9/96–4/98 (33 hours). GPA 3.87.
Surface Search Radar Repair, U.S. Navy, 7/97 (120 hours). Graduated 1 of 4.
Digital Interrogation System Repair, U.S. Navy, 2/93 (680 hours). Graduated 2 of 9.
Electronics Technician School, U.S. Navy, 9/92 (1120 hours).

TERRY F. HEEBERGER

54321 West Lakeview
Pirie, OH 55555
(330) 555-5575
tfheeb@aol.com

Objective and Qualifications

Qualified for supervisory / management positions in production, manufacturing, or distribution. Highlights:

- **Team leader / department supervisor:** More than six years of supervisory experience in shipping, receiving, and warehousing, with record of exceeding goals for productivity, cost-containment, and quality.
- **Company-minded and self-directed:** Noted by management for initiative, analytical skills, and ability to develop and motivate team members in union environment.
- **Training:** Bachelor's degree included courses in business, computer literacy, marketing, public relations, and communications. Selected for company-sponsored management training. Computer skills include MS Excel, MS Word, e-mail, and Internet navigation.

Experience

WALGREEN'S DISTRIBUTION CENTER
11/91-Present
1.8 million square-foot center ships 36 million cartons annually, supplying 300 stores in a four-state area.

Supervisor

Cross-trained in and supervised various departments, including Repack, Quality Assurance, JIT, Put Away, Accelerated Flow-Through, and Case Pack. Currently perform responsibilities of an Operations Manager on second shift, ensuring key Case Pack department runs productively, safely, and cost-effectively. Direct a crew of 21-26 warehouse laborers, with responsibility for employee development, evaluation, discipline, and dismissals. Control $38 million labor and operating budget. Monitor manhour-to-volume ratios.

Team Contributions

- Increased productivity from 22 to 28.5 cartons per manhour—highest among 14 centers in the nation.
- Exceeded cubilization goal 10%—from 80% to 90% cubic feet per shipment—in Case Pack department.
- Increased order fill rate from 98.5% to 99.5%.
- Saved approximately $3.5 million in labor expenses in prior fiscal year; virtually eliminated overtime.
- Improved productivity from 12 to 15 pallets per hour in Put Away department.
- Helped implement WICS inventory control system for Accelerated Flow-Through department, improving turnaround on unloading-storage-reshipment of merchandise from 1 week to 24 hours.

Other Achievements

- Promoted from laborer to supervisor in 18 months—normal advancement track is 3-4 years.
- Frequently assigned by management to turn around problem areas.
- Selected to troubleshoot and operate key equipment to ensure optimum merchandise flow through system.

Education

BALL STATE UNIVERSITY
Bachelor of Science degree, Business Administration, 1991

CHAPTER

7

Writing a
Winning Resume

The Edge resume system makes a distinction between (1) the basic writing of a resume and (2) the design and presentation of that resume. Previous chapters have stressed uniqueness of *approach*. However, one comedian's comment about a popular book is very appropriate here: "It doesn't matter what color your parachute is if it doesn't open." In other words, the *content* of your resume is its most important feature. No amount of clever presentation will overcome a poorly organized, poorly written resume.

We present this chapter for those either starting the resume-writing process or those willing to take a hard look at their present resumes. Frankly, a large percentage of current resumes are seriously flawed: poorly organized, too long, too short, misdirected in terms of emphasis, or incorrect in terms of grammar and spelling.

Why You Might *Not* Want to Use This Chapter

There are, however, two potential reasons for skipping this chapter. First, if your resume is current and unquestionably well-crafted, there is no need to reinvent the wheel. You might browse this section for new ideas, but you primarily will use the Edge to craft a unique presentation of your current resume content.

Second, you might want to work directly with a resume-writing expert. Without question, there are professional resume consultants who have excellent approaches to word-crafting. We are gratified that many of these professionals have embraced our concept, realizing that in today's competitive marketplace, an Edge is necessary—and that our approach is compatible with, not competitive with, their role as professionals.

For example, the Professional Association of Resume Writers (PARW) has recommended the Edge strategy as a powerful tool for individual resume writers. This national association consists of professionals who are kept up-to-date with current resume-writing techniques and job-search strategies. Many of its members offer a broad range of job-search services, including cover letter preparation, interview coaching, and follow-up techniques.

To find the closest PARW member in your area, look in your yellow pages for the PARW logo or visit the Web site at www.parw.com. If you are a resume writer or career consultant and are interested in joining PARW, you can find membership information on their Web site, or call 800-822-7279.

For those of you who are going to craft your own resumes, however, this chapter presents a compilation of essential resume-writing guidelines and concepts.

A Quick Word About Writer's Block

Professional writers occasionally experience a strange paralysis known as writer's block. For some reason, the words just won't come. The words that do come are not the words you want. And the wastebasket (electronic or metal) is soon full of discarded starts. A variation of this malady often attacks the resume writer. You find it very hard to decide which experiences are most relevant. You find it hard to find a balance between confidently presenting your skills and sounding like a braggart. You have trouble deciding how much to tailor the resume to specific job possibilities. So you struggle.

Realize that virtually every resume writer experiences this agony. It is one of the key reasons to consider using professional help. Those going it alone often find the best approach is

- Try it today.

- Sleep on it overnight.

- Be prepared to make major edits of your own work and try for draft 2.

- And so on, until complete.

In summary, it is not at all likely that you'll create your final draft in one or even two writing sessions.

Resume Formats

A perusal of most resume-writing books can lead to the terrifying conclusion that there are 101 formats from which to choose. Actually, there are only three basic formats:

1. Chronological

2. Functional

3. Combination of functional/chronological, sometimes called *chrono-functional*

Let's look at each of these standard formats in detail.

Chronological

The chronological resume is a virtual time line, plotting your education and career in reverse chronological order. Some of the people reading resumes have apparently attended a course called "Investigative Resume Reading," where they learned to find gaps in applicants' experiences. Occasionally, no doubt, they uncover a prison term or other career embarrassment, but we suspect the exercise is just one way to add a bit of structure to the very subjective job of resume review. In any case, it is important enough that most resumes should account for the majority of our adult years on Earth. Obviously, the chronological resume is the simplest format to meet this objective.

From the standpoint of the resume writer, this format is most applicable if

- Your career path demonstrates a set of experiences directly relevant to the position being pursued.

- The progression of your career shows the kind of steady advancement that indicates you are a career winner.

Sample—Chronological Format

MICHAEL E. OLSON

4748 East 84th Street

New York, New York 10036

(212) 555-0090

SUMMARY OF QUALIFICATIONS

- Outstanding track record of marketing accomplishments, including product development, new market penetration, and advertising and sales promotion.
- Widely experienced in profit and loss, training and supervision, and public relations.
- Creator of numerous and successful telemarketing, direct mail, and trade show exhibit programs.
- Results-oriented executive combining problem-solving analytical skills with a strong creative flair.

CAREER HISTORY

OMNICOM, *New York, New York*
Director, Market Research, April 1999–Present
Major Clients: Gillette, Polaroid, Du Pont, Avon, Walgreen's, General Electric, Pillsbury, Holiday Inn

- Established and directed all facilities of agency's marketing research department.
- Successfully developed the marketing research function into a profit center.
- Interpreted marketing research and recommendations to improve the quality of client decision making.
- Developed a new approach to reporting and interpreting consumer change for management.

BAUSCH & LOMB, NEW PRODUCTS DIVISION, *Rochester, New York*
Marketing Manager, May 1994–March 1999

- Conceptualized new product designs in current product, which were adopted by management, yielding increased sales of $250,000.
- Introduced product line to new market segments, resulting in multiple purchases and a $300,000 improvement in sales.
- Created and facilitated product seminars for customers and prospects.
- Coordinated and conducted training of sales representatives and managers, leading to $425,000 increase in sales.

PREMARK INTERNATIONAL, HOUSEHOLD PRODUCTS DIVISION, *Deerfield, Illinois*
Marketing Research Services Manager, May 1990–April 1994
Marketing Research Brand Manager, July 1986–April 1990

- Planned and conducted all marketing research for new consumer household products from idea conception through test market.
- Initiated new products team approach by successfully collaborating with members of virtually every corporate group while conducting several new product projects at various stages of development.
- Hired and trained a research assistant and set up a research library.

EDUCATION

Columbia University, *New York, New York*
M.B.A., Marketing, 2001

University of Illinois, *Champaign, Illinois*
B.B.A., Marketing, 1986

The number of positions and career jumps you've made are appropriate at this stage of your career.

To reverse the logic, if your experience isn't directly relevant to the position you're pursuing, your career hasn't progressed logically, or you have hopscotched all over the industry, the chronological format is almost certainly not best.

Remember to stress accomplishments instead of simply printing your job description. Although it's important to every resume format, this kind of information is probably most critical to the chronological resume. Programs implemented, problems solved, numbers achieved—these are the details that show your professional development over time and sell your talent.

> "*Some of the people reading resumes have apparently attended a course called 'Investigative Resume Reading'...*"

Functional

The functional resume places its emphasis on your bank of experiences relevant to the position you are pursuing. This format places much less emphasis on specific employers and dates and more emphasis on the skills and talents you've developed during your working years.

Your employment history is still important in this format, but you place it near the end of your resume. To describe your employment history, you simply list the dates, employer names, and positions you've held. You don't detail your responsibilities in the "history" part of the resume.

The functional resume is very common in today's job market because of the large numbers of people making significant career adjustments—retirees returning to work or people in mid-career who want or need to shift to a new career due to downsizing, lifestyle changes, mergers, or closings. For some, these adjustments involve convincing someone in another industry that your skills are transferable. Others are attempting

HELEN M. YOUNG
3003 North Lincoln Avenue
Indianapolis, IN 46208
(317) 555-7900
E-mail: hmyoung@myemail.com

AREAS OF ACHIEVEMENT

Public Relations

Coordinated and established an Information/Media Center in the Republic of the Philippines. Initiated and wrote press releases, answered queries, and directed photo opportunities.

Provided positive publicity in Japan for the American community on nationwide and local Japanese television.

Established ongoing working rapport with the American Embassy and the International Press Center in Japan and the Republic of the Philippines.

Communications

Initiated on-camera media training for CEOs.

Spoke for the Navy in Washington, D.C., concerning a wide variety of issues with leading national and international media representatives. Participated on an education steering committee related to an HIV/AIDS education film to be distributed Navy-wide.

Developed and executed comprehensive training programs from concept to delivery. Instructed 2,000 U.S. and foreign public relations students annually in the area of public relations, media relations, internal information, electronic news gathering, editing, and planning.

Arranged, organized, and conducted tours, sporting events, and social functions for the internal audience, general public, and media representatives in 12 countries with participation ranging from 2 to 12,000.

Management

Supervised the daily performance of four separate public relations offices that solved public relations problems in the U.S. and overseas.

Prepared the budgets for five different offices.

Recruited and trained more than 55 employees.

Coordinated purchasing for offices of 75 staff.

EMPLOYMENT HISTORY

1999–Present   *Assistant Professor*
Defense Information School, Fort Benjamin Harrison, Indianapolis, Indiana

1995–1999   *Public Affairs Officer*
Navy Bureau of Medicine & Surgery, Washington, D.C.

1993–1994   *Media Officer*
Bureau of Navy Information, The Pentagon, Washington, D.C.

1991–1992   *Director—Speakers Bureau*
Bureau of Navy Information, The Pentagon, Washington, D.C.

1986–1990   *Public Affairs Officer*
Naval Security Group Activity, Misawa, Japan

EDUCATION

Butler University, *Indianapolis, Indiana*
Master of Arts, Communication, 1986

University of Illinois, *Champaign, Illinois*
Bachelor of Science, Public Relations, 1984

CERTIFICATES OF COMPLETION

Defense Information School, *Indianapolis, Indiana*
- *Public Affairs Officer Course, 1986*
- *Electronic News Gathering and Editing Techniques, 1986*
- *Television Production, 1986*

jumps into new job categories. In either case, the functional resume is the most powerful way to present your strengths. You use this format to stress the skills you possess and to assure the prospective employer that your skills are transferable to the new situation.

Combination, or Chrono-Functional

The combination resume typically begins as a functional resume by listing those skills that are most significant to the job you're pursuing. Next, you describe your work history, listing the companies in reverse chronological order. Each listing also includes a description of your responsibilities and achievements with that employer.

This resume format is the choice of upwardly mobile professionals who are on the fast track in a particular career or industry and who want to put equal emphasis on their successful career track and their skills. Typically, this format is not used by those who have less than 12 to 15 years in the workforce.

Resume Elements

As we mentioned earlier, you might need to prepare multiple versions of your resume. For each of these versions, you are likely to choose a different format *and* different elements. The following sections discuss a full range of resume elements. You may never include some of these elements in any of your resumes (in fact, we don't recommend some of them, except under unusual circumstances), but you'll be better able to make choices when you understand how each of them is used.

"A Rose by Any Other Name..."

In the interest of presenting a more complete work regarding resume writing, we briefly cover the subject of properly presenting your name. Seriously, there are some issues to keep in mind.

Sample—Combination Format

LAURA DOBBS
8565 North Oak Street
Indianapolis, Indiana 46260
(317) 555-6500
laura_dobbs@myemail.com

SUMMARY

- Fifteen years accounting experience with a strong background in auditing, business and individual taxes, and cost-control programs.
- Excellent management skills. Consistently obtain high productivity from employees.
- Efficient in implementing computerized accounting systems and designing more effective manual systems.
- Rapidly recognize and analyze company problems and solutions.

EDUCATION

Certified Public Accountant, 1991
Indiana State Certification

Indiana University, Bloomington, Indiana
Bachelor of Science, 1986
Major: Accounting; *Minor:* Business Administration

PROFESSIONAL EXPERIENCE

Cost Accounting
- Developed a major cost-control program that cut overhead 150 percent.
- Reduced costs for small businesses and large corporations.
- Established complete integrated accounting packages for entire corporations.

Accounting and Budgeting
- Designed, installed, and implemented effective budgeting systems under cash and accrual accounting methods.
- Established accounting procedures that significantly reduced errors and duplication of effort by 55 percent.
- Tracked and reduced costs for multimillion–dollar contracts.

Auditing
- Performed audits and developed financial statements for a wide variety of clients.
- Audited multimillion–dollar subcontractors' accounting records and facilities for government contracts.
- Trained employees to comply with new state accounting regulations and identified accounting and operational irregularities.

Management and Administration
- Hired, trained, and managed 5–40 employees.
- Set up and conducted monthly motivational staff meetings.

Extensively involved in customer relations, establishing credit ratings, approving credit, reviewing and approving customer claims, and making collections.

EMPLOYMENT HISTORY

1999–Present   *Controller,* **Indiana Bell,** *Indianapolis, Indiana*
Developed a major cost-control program that cut overhead 15 percent. Trained employees to comply with new state accounting regulations and identified accounting and operations irregularities.

1992–1999   *Controller,* **Cummins Engine,** *Columbus, Indiana*
Established complete integrated accounting package for entire corporation. Developed accounting procedures that reduced errors and duplication of effort by 55 percent.

1986–1992   *Staff Accountant,* **Arthur Andersen & Co.,** *Indianapolis, Indiana*
Converted manual accounting systems to efficient computerized office systems for several companies in Indianapolis. Designed, installed, and implemented effective budgeting systems under cash and accrual accounting methods.

Normally, it looks and works best to state your first name, middle initial, and last name (for example, Susan J. Miller). An exception arises for those whose parents gave them a first name that they have long since ducked (such as Winfield). In this case, the resume may appropriately read "W. Scott Montgomery."

Even if your friends call you Susie or Bill or Jack, it is usually better to use only the formal name "Susan J. Miller" rather than Susie Miller or Susan "Susie" J. Miller. An exception might be appropriate if your name is well known in the industry. For example, Babe Ruth surely didn't use George Herman Ruth on his resume.

In most cases, it's best to have no more than one initial in the name. Susan J. is almost certainly better than S.J. Miller. It is usually unnecessary to write out your full middle name, unless you are called by both your first and middle names (for example, Gloria Jean or John David).

Be aware that married women might want to include their maiden names to more easily facilitate reference checking, such as Mary (Johnson) McCoy.

Contact Information

Because an offer to interview is rarely granted by mail, you must include your full telephone number on the line below your address; many people also list an e-mail address. Ideally, you should list day and evening contact numbers, but all resume readers are aware that your job search might be confidential and a work number might not be practical. With the proliferation of cell phones, pagers, fax machines, and so on, contact number listings could get out of hand! Just remember that work phone, fax, and e-mail addresses can be listed but are optional. If you list only a daytime phone number (and you don't intend to stay by your phone all day), you should invest in an answering machine. Few employers will keep trying to call if they get no answer after a few attempts.

Dates

You can use any of several formats for presenting dates. The most important issue is consistency throughout your resume:

January 2000–December 2004
January 2, 2000–December 31, 2004
1/00–12/04
1/2/00–12/31/04

Objectives

Resume books agonize at length over whether to state an objective and, if so, how.

Resume readers chuckle at the transparent attempts of writers to construct an objective that sounds like your lifelong dream has been to work in Acme Manufacturing's computer department.

Resume printers smile all the way to the bank when resume writers print three different versions of their resume, differing only in the statement of objective.

This advice seems safe: If an objective sounds fluffy, skip it. For example, none of these objectives is worth including on a resume:

OBJECTIVE: To become part of a dynamic company that appreciates and rewards excellent effort.

OBJECTIVE: To obtain a challenging position with a progressive company that can use my experiences and my liberal arts education.

OBJECTIVE: To obtain a challenging position with a progressive company that can offer me the opportunity for advancement.

Similarly, if you are obviously applying for a job in the public relations department of a dynamic company, it seems unnecessary to state

OBJECTIVE: To contribute positively to the public relations effort of a dynamic company.

In almost every case, a far better way to communicate your objectives is in your cover letter; for example, write "I am seeking an opportunity to grow in the field of public relations and feel confident there is an excellent fit between your needs and my skills…."

After having read hundreds of resumes and having spoken to many hiring authorities, we have learned that the majority of people today omit objectives from their resumes. The exception to this may be the scannable resume. Some resume-scanning programs include objectives in their data fields, giving you another "hit" opportunity. (We talk more about scannable resumes in chapter 8.)

> "*Because your resume is likely to be in heavy competition for attention, the summary is an excellent means of grabbing attention.*"

If you choose to use an objective in your resume, make sure that you state it clearly and that it fits perfectly with the position for which you're applying:

OBJECTIVE: A senior-level position in educational software marketing.

For a scannable resume, the same objective might read

OBJECTIVE: A position as Brand Manager, Software Marketing Manager, or similar senior-level appointment.

Those interested in differentiating their resume with the use of Edge humor can certainly use the objective for this purpose:

OBJECTIVE: To get a better job so my wife gets off my back.

OBJECTIVE: Getting someone to realize that my skills are great, my work ethic is excellent, and I'm the ideal person for this job.

Summary

A summary is a list of three to five highlights of your achievements and qualifications that should precede your work history or functional skills. Because your resume is likely to be in heavy competition for attention, the summary is an excellent means of grabbing attention and inspiring the reader to carefully review the rest of your qualifications.

Typical summaries might be

- Effective problem solver using excellent written and verbal communication skills

- Excellent track record for generating overall cost reduction and operation efficiency improvements

- M.B.A. from Indiana University in Business Management

- Strong leadership skills while advancing a team player approach

- 10 years as a proven sales leader with an excellent record of achievement

- Confident, professional communicator with outstanding presentation skills

- Special talent for identifying clients' needs and presenting effective solutions

- Dependable, flexible, and able to maintain a sense of humor under pressure

- Successfully managed budgets in excess of $2 million

- Outstanding management skills while overseeing more than 60 employees

- Experienced in developing short- and long-term financial business planning

- Positive motivator, combining creativity with strong verbal and writing skills

Here is a list of powerful words and phrases that will describe the qualities you might want to emphasize in your summary or anywhere in your resume.

ABILITY TO…	EFFICIENT	PROBLEM SOLVER
ACCOMPLISHED IN…	ENERGETIC	PROFESSIONAL
ACCURATE	ENTHUSIASTIC	PROFICIENT
ACHIEVED	EXCELLENT	PROFITABLY
ADEPT	EXCEPTIONAL	PROVEN
AGGRESSIVE	EXPERIENCED	QUICK
ANALYTICAL	EXTENSIVE	READILY
ASSERTIVE	EXTREMELY	RELIABLE
ATTENTION TO DETAIL	FLEXIBLE	RESPONSIBLE
CHALLENGING	FOLLOW THROUGH	SELF-MOTIVATED
COMMITTED TO…	TO COMPLETION	SENSE OF HUMOR
COMMUNICATION SKILLS	GOAL ACHIEVER	SHARP
COMPETENT	HIGHLY	SPECIAL TALENT
COMPETITIVE	INDUSTRIOUS	STRONG
CONSISTENT	INTERPERSONAL SKILLS	SUCCESSFUL
CREATIVE	KNOWLEDGEABLE	TACTFUL
DECISIVE	LEADERSHIP	TAKE DIRECTIONS
DEDICATED TO…	LEARN QUICKLY	TEAM PLAYER
DEMONSTRATED	MEET DEADLINES	THOROUGH
DEPENDABLE	MOTIVATED	THRIVE ON…
DETAIL-ORIENTED	OBJECTIVE	TRUST
DILIGENT	ORGANIZED	UNDER PRESSURE
DIPLOMATIC	ORIGINAL	UNDERSTANDING
EASILY	OUTSTANDING	UNIQUE
EFFECTIVE	POSITIVE ATTITUDE	VERSATILE

Skills and Experience

When describing your skills and experience, you need to draw on both your writing talents *and* your personal integrity. You can depend on the fact that your resume will be in competition with some written by skillful workers—and others written by skillful fibbers. Although you absolutely must put the best possible light on your accomplishments, you need to do so within the bounds of truthfulness.

Some people who "directed the activity of 150 people" were simply chairman of the company picnic committee. This kind of boldfaced puffery is likely to backfire. Here are some guidelines to remember when describing your skills and experience:

- Describe your successes and accomplishments with creativity and confidence.

- Avoid simply listing your duties as if you were writing a company job description for your boss.

- Avoid any negative words or descriptions.

- Avoid using industry jargon and flowery words the reader might not understand. (For scannable resumes, jargon and acronyms are acceptable if you also define potentially unrecognizable terms.)

- Incorporate numbers, percentages, and statistics into your descriptions when you can.

- Keep your sentences short and to the point. Lengthy, convoluted sentences will sound like intentional mumbo-jumbo.

- Avoid using the pronoun "I." Write in abbreviated third person. Instead of writing "I recruited, trained, and coordinated the activities of 10,000 volunteers," try writing "Recruited, trained, and coordinated activities of 10,000 volunteers."

One way to make your achievements really stand out in your resume is to describe them with effective verbs or action words. On the following page is a list of action words that have been proven to be effective in resumes.

Education

When you list your educational experience, always spell out the name of the degree and the area of specialization; for example, list "Master of Science, Biology" rather than a simple "M.S." In the same vein, spell out the name of your alma mater. Although everyone may know what "UCLA" stands for, take the effort to spell it out. (As you will see in chapter 8, this rule doesn't carry through to scannable resumes, where acronyms for degrees are recommended.)

ACCELERATED	ACCOMPLISHED	ACHIEVED	ACTED
ADAPTED	ADDED	ADDRESSED	ADMINISTERED
ADVANCED	ADVISED	ALLOCATED	ANALYZED
APPRAISED	APPROVED	ARRANGED	ASSEMBLED
ASSIGNED	ASSISTED	ATTAINED	AUDITED
AUTHORED	AUTOMATED	BALANCED	BROADENED
BUDGETED	BUILT	CALCULATED	CATALOGUED
CHAIRED	CHANGED	CLARIFIED	CLASSIFIED
COACHED	COLLECTED	COMPILED	COMPLETED
COMPOSED	COMPUTED	CONCEIVED	CONCEPTUALIZED
CONDUCTED	CONFERRED	CONFRONTED	CONSOLIDATED
CONSTRUCTED	CONTRACTED	CONTRIBUTED	CONTROLLED
CONVERTED	COORDINATED	CORRESPONDED	COUNSELED
CREATED	CRITIQUED	CUT	DECIDED
DECREASED	DELEGATED	DELIVERED	DEMONSTRATED
DERIVED	DESIGNED	DETERMINED	DEVELOPED
DEVISED	DIRECTED	DISPATCHED	DISPENSED
DISPLAYED	DISTINGUISHED	DISTRIBUTED	DIVERSIFIED
DOUBLED	DRAFTED	DRAMATIZED	EARNED
EDITED	EDUCATED	EFFECTED	ELIMINATED
ENABLED	ENCOURAGED	ENGINEERED	ENLISTED
ESTABLISHED	ESTIMATED	EVALUATED	EXAMINED
EXECUTED	EXHIBITED	EXPANDED	EXPEDITED
EXPLAINED	EXPRESSED	EXTRACTED	FABRICATED
FACILITATED	FAMILIARIZED	FASHIONED	FOCUSED
FORECASTED	FORMULATED	FOUNDED	GAINED
GENERATED	GUIDED	HALVED	HANDLED
IDENTIFIED	ILLUSTRATED	IMAGINED	IMPLEMENTED
IMPROVED	INCREASED	INDOCTRINATED	INFLUENCED
INFORMED	INITIATED	INNOVATED	INSPECTED
INSTALLED	INSTITUTED	INSTRUCTED	INTEGRATED
INTERPRETED	INTERVIEWED	INTRODUCED	INVENTED
INVESTIGATED	LAUNCHED	LECTURED	LED
LOCATED	MADE	MAINTAINED	MANAGED
MARKETED	MEASURED	MEDIATED	MODERATED
MONITORED	MOTIVATED	NARRATED	NEGOTIATED
OPERATED	ORGANIZED	ORIGINATED	OVERHAULED
OVERSAW	PARTICIPATED	PERFORMED	PERSUADED
PINPOINTED	PLANNED	PREDICTED	PREPARED
PRESENTED	PRIORITIZED	PROCESSED	PRODUCED
PROGRAMMED	PROJECTED	PROMOTED	PROPOSED
PROVIDED	PUBLICIZED	PUBLISHED	PURCHASED
RAISED	REALIZED	RECOMMENDED	RECONCILED
RECORDED	RECRUITED	REDESIGNED	REDUCED
REFERRED	REGULATED	REHABILITATED	REINFORCED
REMODELED	REORGANIZED	REPAIRED	REPRESENTED
RESEARCHED	RESOLVED	RESTORED	RESTRUCTURED
RETRIEVED	REVAMPED	REVERSED	REVIEWED
REVISED	REVITALIZED	SAVED	SCHEDULED
SCREENED	SELECTED	SERVED	SERVICED
SHAPED	SIMPLIFIED	SKETCHED	SOLD
SOLIDIFIED	SOLVED	SPARKED	SPOKE
SPECIFIED	STAFFED	STARTED	STIMULATED
STRATEGIZED	STREAMLINED	STRENGTHENED	STRESSED
STRETCHED	STRUCTURED	SUCCEEDED	SUMMARIZED
SUPERVISED	SURVEYED	SYSTEMIZED	TABULATED
TAUGHT	TESTED	TRACED	TRACKED
TRAINED	TRANSFERRED	TRANSFORMED	TRANSLATED
TRAVELED	TRIMMED	TURNED	UNCOVERED
UNIFIED	UPDATED	UPGRADED	UTILIZED
VALIDATED	VERIFIED	VISUALIZED	WIDENED
WON	WORKED		

If you are a recent high school graduate, you will want to list the high school you attended, the city, and the year you graduated:

North Central High School, 2000
Indianapolis, Indiana

College graduates need not list high school graduation unless they have just graduated from college and have extremely limited relevant job experience.

Regardless of the degrees you have attained, you will always list them in reverse chronological order:

Butler University, Indianapolis, Indiana
Master of Business Administration, 2001

DePauw University, Greencastle, Indiana
Bachelor of Arts in Economics, 1996

If you attended college but didn't graduate, you will want to list the college and city, but don't list the date you would have graduated or the degree you would have received. It is acceptable to list your major or emphasis in school:

Indiana University, Bloomington, Indiana
Major: Computer Science

Where to place your education depends on many factors: your years of experience, your level of education, and the relevance of your education to the position you are pursuing. The following list gives recommended placement for your education, based on its relevance to the position you're seeking:

1. If your education is pertinent to the position you are pursuing (a master's degree, a doctorate, or an education certification), list it in reverse chronological order before you state your experience or skills.

2. If your education is not pertinent to the position you are pursuing, but it is a degree of higher education and you have less than 15 years of experience, we suggest that you list it before you state your work experience or functional skills.

3. If you have more than 15 years of experience and your degree is not directly relevant to the position you seek, you will want to list your education toward the end of your resume.

Activities and Professional Affiliations

Listing irrelevant hobbies and organizational affiliations can actually backfire. "Why would I care that he plays tournament chess?" "Anybody who goes skydiving is too much of a risk-taker!" "If she belongs to that organization, she may be a wild-eyed liberal!" On the other hand, well-chosen listings can demonstrate that you are a well-rounded person, a person involved in your community, or a person advancing career knowledge outside the workplace.

Again, be aware of potential reaction and ask for input from objective advisors. As a guideline, list interests and affiliations only if they meet at least three of these criteria:

- You have been a member of this organization within the past five years.

- You are or were an active member.

- The organization relates to your career choice.

- The activity is generally held to be healthful, wholesome, or otherwise positive.

- The activity will not offend or look silly to the reader.

Current or Previous Salaries

It is almost never advisable to list your salary demand on your resume. You risk sounding either overpriced or underpriced. You risk the reader jumping to conclusions about the salary level you would or would not accept despite the

> "*It is almost never advisable to list your salary demand on your resume.*"

possibility that the benefits may make a lower base salary desirable. In general, it's best to negotiate salary further down the interviewing road.

If an application specifically requests salary history, you must use your cover letter to anticipate possible communication problems and deal with them:

- "Although my previous job was at a level of $37,000, I am far more interested in a satisfying job than a specific income figure."

- "Frankly, I know I'm worth considerably more than my present income level, and this confidence is the primary reason I'm interested in this position."

- "I hope we can discuss the income issue face-to-face. My previous employer did not offer some benefits that your company makes available. I'm well aware that these factors are just as important as monthly wages."

- "Within the past five years, I have been earning between $30,000 and $33,000, in addition to various benefit programs. However, I would appreciate the opportunity to discuss with you a compensation plan relevant to the position of Brand Manager at XYZ Products, Inc."

References

It is almost never necessary to include references on the resume. They take valuable space, and the interviewer will not need them until you've survived initial screening and, probably, an initial interview. Equally unnecessary is the often-used statement "References available upon request." It's an obvious truth, so why waste space on the resume to state it?

An exception to the "no listed references" rule might be a professional reference of such weight that the opportunity to "name drop" might be helpful in grabbing the reader's attention. Examples are widely known industry figures, public figures, or critics.

At some point in the interviewing process, your references will become crucial. Most likely to be checked are professional references. Make sure that you choose references who represent people within your profession or those who have known you in an educational or work environment for an extended period of time. Most interviewers assume your mother, pastor, and close friends think well of you.

Reasons for Leaving Previous or Current Positions

It is almost never advisable for your resume to list reasons for departing prior employment. These can be discussed during an interview. In some cases, they may be appropriate for discussion in your cover letter—but the resume should remain positive.

Age, Race, Religion, Sex, or National Origin

Equal Employment Opportunity laws state that it is illegal to hire, fire, or refuse an interview for employment based on age, race, religion, sex, or national origin. Thus, it is unnecessary to list those descriptions of yourself.

As a practical matter, many companies are attempting to balance their workforce to remedy past discrimination. If you are aware that a company is attempting to add more of whatever you are, you may be able to list affiliations, references to dates, or other information that is informative but not blatant. This step is perfectly legal. The company cannot ask you to list such information, but you are within the law to volunteer it.

Personal Information

Personal information is data such as height, weight, health status, marital status, number of children, names and ages of family members, and personal likes and dislikes. The resume industry is in major discord on this issue. Obviously, the same anti-discrimination laws just mentioned preclude an employer from hiring based on most items of personal information. In fact, it is currently illegal for an interviewer to ask about a person's marital status, child count, and plans for having children. In most cases, you are wise to omit the personal section of your resume.

As we discussed earlier, however, the specific job or industry to which you are applying may dictate that you include personal information. For example, if you are applying for a job that would, for whatever reason, favor someone who is 6′4″ and weighs 220, then mention it. If you know that a company has a strong stance on family values, mention your family. Use your own judgment—and your company and industry research—when making this call.

Finally, we should mention that the personal section provides another opportunity for demonstrating your sense of humor. An Edge associate created a resume that was a real keeper with this personal section:

PERSONAL:

Height: 6′2″	Health: Excellent
Weight: 190 lbs.	Hat Size: 7
Single	Shoe Size: 11$\frac{1}{2}$
No Children	Tennis Shoe: Nike

Photographs

The advice concerning photographs is similar to the previous discussions. It is not necessary, it is certainly not common, and in most cases, it's a mistake. Including a photo is risky in the sense that a reader might not "like your looks" for whatever reason. However, if some unique aspect of yourself is best communicated with a photograph, and if you (and your objective advisors) believe the photograph clearly gives you an Edge, it is acceptable.

If you do decide to use a photograph, the print quality must be excellent. Photo quality varies dramatically among printing processes and among printing companies. Be sure your company can do an excellent job.

One creative resume idea (almost over the Edge) was built around a head-to-foot photograph of an applicant with captions surrounding the photograph, such as the following:

"Eyes that see the future with vision."

"Sleeves that are rolled up, ready for hard work."

Endorsements

An endorsement is a quote from an associate or boss that describes your attributes or successes in a previous or current job. The endorsement is appropriate as part of a job description or functional skill description. An example of an endorsement follows:

Facilitated weeklong courses on substance abuse prevention. Spoke before numerous community groups on family mental health issues. Excellent ability to entertain the audience while educating them on important topics.

(The Boss, XYZ Company)

Using one or two endorsements if space allows can enhance your resume. Using more than two endorsements can make you or your resume appear self-exalting.

Resume Length

The length of your resume involves these considerations:

- Other things being equal, it is best that your resume not exceed one page. This guideline is simply a bow to the reality that attention is hard to get. And attention to a lengthy resume is not likely. Desktop publishing technology, which allows easy change of type styles and type sizes, helps fit more information on a single page.

- However, if your career spans more than 20 years or you are applying for very high-level positions, it is arguable that you might have accumulated too much experience to fit onto a single page. In this case, work hard to create summaries and other attention-grabbing devices that inspire your reader to wade through the longer resume.

If your resume should fit one page but presently doesn't, you need an editor (yourself or your objective advisor) to ask these questions:

- Is some of the information just plain irrelevant?

- Can some of the early job positions be eliminated or combined because they're not as meaningful as more recent information?

- Can some of your verbiage be trimmed of fat?

- Can you use a different format that doesn't waste as much space? For example, immense space is wasted by the age-old format of blocking text at the right and putting the single words Experience or Education at the left.

Note: If you are submitting a scannable resume, it's less critical that you keep its length at one page. If you need to use additional pages, make sure you place your name at the top of *every* page and don't staple the pages together. You learn more about scannable resumes in chapter 8.

How Many Different Resumes Do You Need?

Even though elimination of multiple objectives offers a way to reduce the number of resumes you need, it is generally accepted that today's job market demands more than one version of your resume.

One successful Edge associate interviewed for marketing and public relations positions with a functional resume with different emphases on his skills. Another associate used a functional resume to apply for positions outside his immediate industry and a chronological resume to apply within his industry.

Certainly in the Edge strategy, you should consider resumes that are much less traditional when you know your odds of consideration for a specific job are slim unless you dare to be different.

Other Resume-Writing Books

Britton Whitcomb, Susan. *Résumé Magic.* JIST Works, Inc., 8902 Otis Avenue, Indianapolis, IN 46216. 1999.

Farr, J. Michael. *The Quick Resume and Cover Letter Book.* JIST Works, Inc., 8902 Otis Avenue, Indianapolis, IN 46216. 2000.

Kursmark, Louise. *Sales and Marketing Resumes for $100,000 Careers.* JIST Works, Inc., 8902 Otis Avenue, Indianapolis, IN 46216. 2000.

Noble, David. *Gallery of Best Resumes.* JIST Works, Inc., 8902 Otis Avenue, Indianapolis, IN 46216. 1994.

Noble, David. *Gallery of Best Resumes.* JIST Works, Inc., 8902 Otis Avenue, Indianapolis, IN 46216. 1994.

Noble, David. *Gallery of Best Resumes for Two-Year Degree Graduates.* JIST Works, Inc., 8902 Otis Avenue, Indianapolis, IN 46216. 1996.

Noble, David. *Professional Resumes for Accounting, Tax, Finance, and Law.* JIST Works, Inc., 8902 Otis Avenue, Indianapolis, IN 46216. 2000.

Noble, David. *Professional Resumes for Executives, Managers, and Other Administrators.* JIST Works, Inc., 8902 Otis Avenue, Indianapolis, IN 46216. 1998.

Creating Scannable and Electronic Resumes

"Uh, we, uh, we were impressed by your electronic resume, Mr. Zitter, but, uh..."

Given the fast pace and volatility of today's job market, it's not surprising that more of the business of job seeking and job hiring is being conducted on computers. Businesses large and small are turning to the use of electronic and scannable resumes because they provide a cheap, fast, and efficient way to find candidates. As companies advertise jobs online, receive resumes as e-mail attachments, and rely on computers to do the initial resume screening and sorting, job seekers who aren't prepared to play in this arena have a significant disadvantage.

Although the focus of this book isn't online job hunting, you can find ample sources for that information online. Most of the major search engines (such as Yahoo!, Lycos, and InfoSeek) have home-page categories for "Jobs," "Careers," or "Classifieds," where you can find numerous helpful resources for beginning an online search. Those wanting to study this subject in depth might want to read one of the many books available on this subject, including the following:

Criscito, Pat. *Resumes in Cyberspace: Your Complete Guide to a Computerized Job Search*. Barron's Educational Series. 1997.

Nemnich, Mary B. and Fred Jandt. *Cyberspace Job Search Kit,* Third Edition. JIST Works, Inc., 8902 Otis Avenue, Indianapolis, IN 46216. 2000.

Nemnich, Mary B. and Fred Jandt. *Cyberspace Resume Kit.* JIST Works, Inc., 8902 Otis Avenue, Indianapolis, IN 46216. 1999.

Smith, Rebecca. *Electronic Resumes & Online Networking: How to Use the Internet to Do a Better Job Search, Including a Complete, Up-To-Date Resource Guide*. Career Press. 1999.

In this chapter, we focus on giving you the critical information you need about preparing scannable and electronic resumes. First, let's define each of these resume types.

The Basics of Scannable and Electronic Resumes

Scannable resumes serve the same purposes as their traditional counterparts, but they do it in a different way because they're designed for a different audience. Whereas a traditional resume succeeds if it appeals to humans with its eye-catching design and well-phrased descriptions of all the wonderful highlights of the subject's career, a scannable resume has to be read by a computer, so it succeeds if it's clean and properly formatted and carries lots of terms that will catch the "eye" of the computerized scanning software.

The company receives your scannable resume (either on hard copy or as an electronic file) and uses a computer program to scan and move the information into a central database of resumes. There, its contents are searched and sorted based on your qualifications and their appropriateness for available positions. The scannable resume catches the computer's "eye" by containing lots of keywords that name your accomplishments, degrees, jobs held, and so on. The number of appropriate keywords determines whether your resume is placed in—and maybe at the top of!—the right "stack."

A scannable resume, therefore, also must be searchable. To be scannable, the resume must be clean, properly formatted, and presented in the right physical package—which we discuss later. To be *searchable,* the resume must have the right content and list the right keywords to indicate your qualifications for the job you're seeking. If you want (or are asked) to submit your resume electronically, it also must be capable of being transmitted via e-mail or the Internet and then opened and read by a potential employer.

An *electronic* resume is simply a resume sent and stored in the form of an electronic file. Many companies request that applicants submit resumes via the Internet or e-mail, either as an attachment or as an imbedded message. Many of these same companies use the scanning and sorting technology described earlier, so many of the same rules dictate the layout and content of electronic and scannable resumes. Some job hunters post their resumes online, on any of a number of online job placement sites. Online resumes are prime candidates for the services of a resume preparation service. Later in this chapter, you learn more about those services and the details of preparing electronic resumes.

Do You Need a Scannable or Electronic Resume?

The answer is probably "yes." Although these resume formats require some special effort to follow the Edge concept, chances are that many of the prime opportunities you'll be interested in will require one of these resume types. To cover your bases, you can always send two resumes—one scannable or electronic and one hard copy with all of the design and content elements to appeal to the "human eye." Also, if your scannable resume is successful in landing you the interview, you can take along a copy of your traditional resume for the employer's further review. In any case, you don't want (or need) to miss out on any job opportunity because you haven't prepared the required materials. As you'll see, scannable and electronic resumes are *not* difficult to create—and professional help is readily available online or through any resume service.

Designing the Scannable Resume

You needn't be a programmer to understand the reasons behind the design of a good scannable resume, but it doesn't hurt to know the basic process through which a scannable resume passes. Resume search software scans information and sorts it into a database. Database computer applications set up numerous "fields" for the storage of data. For example, a database might have these fields:

[First name] [Middle initial] [Last name] [Address] [City] [State] [Zip]
[College: bachelors] [College: masters] [College: doctorate] [Degree:
bachelors] and so on

Database programs store this data and then sort and retrieve
files according to the requestor's criteria, which are usually based
on keywords. The resumes that contain the keywords relevant to
a given search are then sorted out for further consideration.

Content for Scannable Resumes

To design effective content for a scannable resume, you have to
know the right keywords for the position and industry for which
you're applying. The research you've conducted for your Edge
strategy—your informational interviews, online research, and
readings in industry publications, business analyses, news articles, and so on—will help you identify the terms used to describe positions, activities, and results within your chosen field.

For example, to describe a sales and marketing background,
you'd use such terms as brand management, sales revenue
forecasting, market share, national accounts manager, and so
on. To describe a background as an executive assistant, you
would want to include terms such as multitasking, project management, spreadsheet development, personnel management,
written and oral communication skills, and contract preparation. The higher the number of appropriate keywords you use,
the more "hits" your resume will generate, so you're wise to use
different keywords as often as possible, rather than repeat the
same keywords throughout the resume.

It's also important to use descriptive nouns, such as "accounts
manager," "budget surplus," and "product development"
rather than the action words you may use in the traditional
resume, where you might have said "While managing all of the
company's accounts, I also helped develop a number of products that came in well under budget."

Finally, you actually want to include jargon and educational
details in your scannable resume. Jargon is frequently included
in keyword searches; if you think some jargon may be too

obscure, use it and then spell it out, too. In your educational listing, you *should* use abbreviations such as B.S., M.A., and so on to cite your degrees. You'll gain further database "hits" by listing specific course work, seminars, or special credentials that are key to the industry to which you're applying.

Formatting a Scannable Resume

Follow these general guidelines for formatting your scannable resume:

- Use a standard, sans-serif font (such as Helvetica, Courier, Futura, or Optima) in 11- to 14-point size.

- Left-justify your text, and use all caps for headings.

- Don't use graphic characters, such as hollow bullets, squares, or shadows.

- Don't use tabs, columns, lines, parentheses, brackets, underlining, bold, or other potentially "computer-confusing" graphic effects or elements.

- Don't use line compression.

- Use wide margins.

- Repeat your name at the top of every page; multiple pages are perfectly acceptable, but each must carry your identification.

Finally, you should also follow these "material" guidelines for your scannable resume:

- Use only white (or a very light color) $8^{1}/_{2} \times 11$–inch paper.

- Use only laser-printed originals—no dot matrix and no copies.

- Don't fold your resume; submit hard copy in a flat 9×12–inch envelope.

- Don't use staples to hold together multiple pages.

We show an example of a scannable resume on page 95.

Submitting an Electronic Resume

When you submit an electronic resume, it must be in a file type that can be uploaded or sent via e-mail or the Internet, and then downloaded and read by the recipient. Some employers will clearly state a specific format in which they want to receive electronic files. Some employers even supply on their Web sites a sort of universal electronic resume form, called an *e-form*. You just fill it in and click to return it. The more common method of submitting an electronic resume, however, is as an e-mail attachment. You create the file using your word processing program and then save it in a file format that's most likely to be readable by the majority of systems. Therefore, you should probably use *rich text format* (RTF) or ASCII.

RTF has the advantage of maintaining some file formatting (although scanned resumes won't carry much formatting anyway). To save your file in rich text format, you should prepare your resume in a common word processing program, such as Microsoft Word or WordPerfect, and then use the Save As command to save it in RTF format. In Word, for example, you can save your file as an RTF file by choosing File, Save As and then clicking the Save As Type drop-down arrow and choosing "Rich Text Format (*.rtf)" from the list. Close the file and send it as an e-mail attachment. (See your e-mail program's Help feature if you're uncertain how to do this.)

ASCII doesn't transmit any formatting, but it can be read by PCs, UNIX workstations, Macintosh computers, or mainframe terminals. If you're unsure whether your recipient works with any of the popular word processing programs, ASCII format might be the better choice. To save your resume in this format, make sure you've used flush-left text and no formatting and that you've set your right margin no farther than 6.5. If you prepared it in a word processing program, use the Save As feature to save it as an ASCII text file. You can send this as a text-only e-mail attachment, or you can copy and paste it directly into your e-mail message.

Using an Online Resume Service

If the preceding information has left you feeling a bit over-whelmed or discouraged about your ability to prepare or send electronic and/or scannable resumes, don't despair. As we said earlier, there are a lot of informative resources—both in print and online—to help you with this process. Many online resume services are available to do the job for you. The costs of these services can be quite reasonable, and—given the proliferation of this technology in the job market—an electronic resume might be a tool you can't afford to do without.

The Impact of Technology on the Edge Strategy

As discussed earlier, it is not wise to send a multicolor graphic masterpiece to a computer that thinks in stark black and white. Although this truth impacts the Edge strategy, the overall Edge concept is not affected for some very basic reasons.

Eventually, humans must interact. Computers can handle various screening functions, but computers have no ability to gauge the human qualities that finally determine who will be selected for a job. At some point, you will be contacted, and you will have an opportunity (even if not formally requested) to respond in writing. You can forward a cover letter, which sells you as a person. It might be appropriate to forward your traditional resume. You can certainly forward some kind of creative page summarizing your career or accomplishments. After initial contact, you can use Edge strategies for follow-up notes or letters.

If competing job applicants relax, thinking that responding to a cold computer is the only necessary step, your opportunity to use Edge strategies to stand out might be even better in the electronic world than in the traditional resume world.

CHAPTER

9

Moving Even
Closer to the Edge

John Miller

10 years experience in management,
finance and marketing.

B.S. in Business Management, 1982

Excellent written and verbal
communication skills.

Highly versatile and well organized.

CALL
(312) 555-5000

It is ironic for three reasons that the world of traditional resumes is dry, factual, and gray:

1. As we've stressed throughout this book, your dry, factual, gray resume has little chance of standing out in a huge crowd.

2. A survey of bosses rated "sense of humor" as an extremely important quality in their employees. Yet resumes rarely exhibit this key trait.

3. The poor soul who must read 400 resumes faces deadly boredom. Logically, that person will appreciate some bright spots simply because they break the monotony.

Again, a resume can stand out through simple devices such as color. If you are confident that your words—both resume content and cover letter—make it clear you are an outstanding candidate, you need not consider using more extreme approaches. Even in this case, however, using some relaxed humor can communicate both confidence and creativity:

- "It must be an incredible job reading through the stack of resumes you'll receive for this position. I'd like to think this one can save you some time. When I read your list of qualifications, I said, 'John, this is the job you've spent 15 years getting ready for.'…"

- "When I see an interesting career opportunity, I always make a two-column list: What You Want…What I Offer. The job you listed on Sunday fit so well I almost addressed this letter to 'Dear Glove:'. Seriously, I am excited about the fit. I believe my resume will indicate the extent to which I am ready to tackle this position. And I look forward to the opportunity to meet with you…." (As an idea closer to the Edge, you could use similar wording and enclose a glove.)

> **"A** *survey of bosses rated 'sense of humor' as an extremely important quality in their employees. Yet resumes rarely exhibit this key trait."*

📝 A recent college graduate included this item under Activities: Young Republicans Club (but work well with Democrats, also).

How Close to the Edge Should You Go?

This chapter is intended for those who make this critical assessment:

> These people are going to receive 500 resumes. There is no chance that my pedigree will be in the top 3 percent. If I rely strictly on my background and experience, I will never emerge from the deep stack. Therefore, I have nothing to lose and much to gain by daring to be different.

Note that this assessment is not an indication that you are calling yourself a loser or are otherwise negative about your self-worth. You are simply saying

📝 I've not been in the workforce nearly as long as many other applicants. Their list of credentials will be far longer than mine.

📝 I've worked for a relatively unknown company and will be competing with candidates from more prestigious firms.

📝 These people value Ivy League education highly, and unfortunately, my degree is from Podunk State.

📝 I'm trying to jump from one industry to another; therefore, my credentials will not appear as relevant as those for people who have spent their careers in the industry.

Make no mistake: The Edge isn't a technique designed to help people con their way into a job by using gimmicks. But in many cases, you know you can do a job if you're given a chance. Why not draw upon your creativity to design a resume package that is so unique it will (at least) get you noticed? If you can get the attention of the hiring manager, you may have an opportunity to sell yourself in ways that even the best resume couldn't match.

The balance of this chapter contains ideas of all kinds. We suggest you read through this chapter a couple of times and go to the place (shower or wherever) where your most creative ideas come to you. Perhaps by recruiting people you enjoy brainstorming with, you can come up with your own innovative approach to crafting an "Edgey" resume and cover letter package.

Some of the ideas we show here may require working with a graphic artist. However, all can be executed easily using desktop publishing along with basic drawings or clip art.

Resume Concepts Closer to the Edge

The following list of resume ideas isn't your finite "options list." In fact, although you may decide to use one or more of these ideas in your resume, the list is really intended to help spur your creativity. As you read through these ideas, you undoubtedly will develop your own concepts for Edge resume content. Use them! No one can express your individuality better than you can.

Here are *some* of the ways you can move your resume closer to the Edge:

- Simulate computer paper with holes and perforations printed at the sides of the resume.

- Print a computer with a giant screen on the resume (or cover letter), and then print the content of your resume or cover letter within the screen.

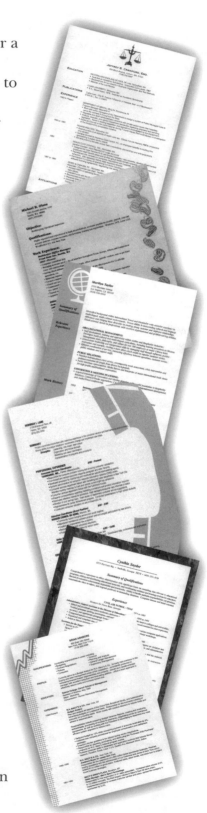

- Illustrate your resume or cover letter with images that support your words. For example, a briefcase, suitcase, miniature dollar bills, miniature contracts, or other designs relevant to your profession might cleverly illustrate these passages:

  > "I realize the job involves heavy travel throughout the eastern seaboard. My suitcase is packed and ready...."

  > "I know my marketing skills will lead to many important contracts for your firm...."

- Use the images of a seed becoming a sprout becoming a full-grown plant or tree as you move through your background and experiences.

- Find a picture of yourself as a child doing something related to the position. Caption it "From an early age, _____ in training to...."

- Print a target in the background of your resume and cover letter with words suggesting that the employer will be "on target" when they hire you. (This requires a printing process called "screening" onto a metal plate. We suggest a 10 percent screen tint.)

- Submit a tiny version of your resume, perhaps 4×6 inches. Clip it to the cover letter with words such as "Throughout my career, I have relentlessly sought ways to improve profitability through reducing cost. My mini-resume indicates this dedication. However, realizing it's a bit hard to read, I've also enclosed a full-size version." (You can probably use desktop publishing equipment to print at a reduced percentage. If it's not legible, a printer can make a *PMT reduction,* which will provide legibility at a tiny size.)

- Also for those demonstrating cost-cutting orientation, print the back of the resume and cover letter with something indicating that the paper has already been used and you are recycling the back side. One sheet could be a memo from a fellow employee, the other a handwritten note from a relative. Words would stress your constant orientation toward cost reduction.

- Submit a jumbo resume, perhaps 17 × 22 inches. This will fold in fourths to fit a 9 × 12 envelope. Use language such as "Knowing that the person you seek must be willing to think big to be successful, I hereby show my willingness! Also for your convenience, I've enclosed a standard version."

- Create (or pay a designer to create) a distinctive logo of your own, perhaps initials built into an industry symbol, which appears on all your material: envelope, cover letter, resume, and follow-up card.

- If working with a strong commercial printer, discuss the use of special decorative techniques. For example, *varnish* is a transparent ink that creates a subtle, shiny highlight where it's printed; you can use varnish wherever you want to add special emphasis on your page. *Embossing*, another popular technique, creates raised or depressed areas on the page, perhaps for a monogram or industry symbol.

- Forward your resume bound to the top of perhaps 20 sheets of plain paper. When the resume is torn off, the reader will have a usable notepad. Explain that you want to be sure your resume is at the top of the stack.

- Print a real or simulated thumbprint with wording about your uniqueness.

- Send a version of your resume cut into perhaps five pieces to create a puzzle. Use wording such as "I'm confident I can solve the 'who to hire' puzzle."

- Use the puzzle idea as a follow-up device. Follow your more traditional resume with a resume cut into pieces. Include a note such as "I continue to be confident I can solve your 'who to hire' puzzle. (Actually, my intact version was forwarded three days ago, but I just wanted to stay in touch!) I look forward to hearing from you...."

- If applying for a position in sales or marketing, use the idea of getting a person to sign her name on the dotted line. For example, in your cover letter, you could write: "I am so oriented toward getting clients to sign on the dotted line, I couldn't help including this concept in my resume. Please sign below...." At the bottom of the page would be something like

Yes, this applicant definitely deserves further consideration.

Signed _____

- Include a blank Post-it Note or a Post-it Note already carrying the line "Excellent candidate; be sure to interview" attached to your resume or cover letter with words such as "I'm so confident of the fit between your needs and my qualifications, I've taken the liberty of enclosing a Post-it Note for your use."

- If money is no object and you're connected in the field of high-end graphic design, consider some kind of pop-up resume.

- Create a resume in a completely different format, such as a brochure.

- If the envelope is likely to be seen by the decision-maker, include art or slogans on the envelope:

    "Resume of an excellent candidate trapped in here; please release and review!"

Using a "Creative" Page

You might want to consider adding to your resume and cover letter package a separate "creative" page, used solely to demonstrate your creativity.

The creative page could include

- Cartoons.

- A gag list of famous people in the field with your name sandwiched between Thomas Watson and Steve Jobs.

- A gag set of endorsements or references, including famous people, living and dead, and relatives.

  > "This lady knows about savings and earnings; dollars and not just pennies." —Benjamin Franklin

  > "She is hardworking, bright, and alert. Definitely a wonderful person for your job opening." —Her mother

- A photo of an old-fashioned sports team or of a team you formerly played on, with a caption such as "Aware of the importance of dedication, hard work, and teamwork."

- A simulated newspaper front page carrying "stories" about your career. *(See page 5.)*

If you use this approach, be sure to reference the creative page in your cover letter.

Video Resumes

Video technology provides a relatively new medium for resumes. You can take advantage of this medium in a few different ways:

- By creating your own videotape, whether home-produced or professionally produced.

- By participating in a video job exchange—an emerging trend on cable channels in various cities.

Two considerations are vital to your decision to create a video resume:

- Your research must indicate that the video will be viewed.

- Your candid self-assessment must confirm that you project better on TV than most of the car dealers who decide to be in their own commercials.

Creating Your Own Web Page

If you have the technical expertise to do it, you may want to consider creating your own Web page and referencing it in your resume/cover letter package. The Web has become a high-traffic area for both job seekers and employers—particularly for those in the field of computer technologies. You can use your own Web page to demonstrate your creativity and technological skill and to give people a closer look at your personal and professional profile. This medium isn't for everyone, however. As with other techniques discussed in this book, you must be confident that you know your industry and the potential employers within that industry well enough to design a site that will work for you (rather than against you).

If you are interested in learning more about building a Web page, you can find numerous online resources. Here are just a few:

The Basic Web Resource Site:
http://website.lineone.net/~alan.duncan/fpe/home.htm

The Pixel Pen:
http://home.earthlink.net/~thomasareed/pixelpen/

Web Pages for Absolute Beginners:
http://subnet.virtual-pc.com/li542871/index.html

CHAPTER

10

Make It a Campaign

For many people, the rational job-search campaign can be described by these steps:

- Hear about an opportunity.

- Mail a resume.

- Wait.

- Wait.

- Wait.

> **"I**t is far more effective to view the job search as a multi-phase campaign."

It is far more effective to view the job search as a multi-phase, proactive campaign. A classic example has become part of the lore of the advertising industry. (We've only slightly fictionalized this true story.)

- In August, the CEO of a large agency receives a wave of postcards announcing "John Miller is coming."

- In September, the wave of postcards continues: "John Miller is coming on October 6."

- On October 5, a billboard across the street blares "John Miller is coming at 9:30 a.m. on Thursday, October 6."

- At 9:20 on October 6, a delivery truck unloads a huge crate, which is carted into the agency's office.

- While a curious crowd, including the CEO, watches, the sides of the crate are dropped, and there, in professional attire at a mini computer workstation, sits John Miller.

- He was hired on the spot.

While perhaps an extreme example, John's approach makes clear that a distinct job search campaign can and should include multiple elements.

At a minimum, we suggest

- Initial resume/cover letter mailing.

- Almost immediate follow-up by phone or a clever mailing to attempt to move the resume to the top of the stack.

- Appropriate thank-yous for

  ▶ Speaking with you by phone

  ▶ Meeting with you

  ▶ Meeting with you for a second interview

- Printed elements of the campaign having a well-defined look or theme, which is included in every piece.

> *"Aggressive follow-up is certainly consistent with the Edge strategy."*

Aggressive follow-up is certainly consistent with the Edge strategy. A resume sitting in a pile of 400 might need an extra boost to reach the top of the stack, so these kinds of ideas will be helpful.

Following Up by Phone

Opinions are divided about aggressively following up by phone. Some job seekers don't do it simply because they are totally uncomfortable with the process. Others, particularly those seeking jobs in the fields of sales and marketing, view personal contact as a natural part of selling themselves. In these fields, failure to follow up might be construed as lack of critical aggressiveness.

Many job announcements clearly state "no phone calls, please" or some other indicator that phone contact is discouraged. But in other cases, you might want to consider following up your resume submission with a phone call. Be brief, stick to the point, and make sure you emphasize the reason you are aggressively pursuing the position. Consider the following examples:

- "Frank, this is Jerome Mitchell. I'm applying for your job in payables. It really looks like my background fits your needs perfectly. I don't want to be overly pushy, but I'll be in your area Tuesday and wondered if I might stop by to meet with you briefly."

● "Mr. Jones, this is Fred Johnson. Our mutual friend Jim Jackson told me about your opening in sales and thought my background as a 14-year veteran of sales management would be perfect. Might I stop by for a few minutes to discuss the possibility?"

● "Miss Marshall, this is Peggy McConnell. I know your formal application system is probably by mail, but I'm so excited about the opportunity you're offering that I wanted to call and see if I could arrange an interview. Your job fits my skills exactly. Would you be willing to see me for a few minutes?"

Following Up in Person

Even more aggressive than a phone call is simply showing up at the target office. At worst, you can drop off a resume. With luck, some discussion with the person in the reception office, and perhaps a bit of dancing and singing, you might wrangle a brief interview. Here are some sample "approaches" that could be used in such a follow-up:

● "Mary, I know Mr. Smith is busy and he may insist on prior appointments, but do you suppose there's any chance he'd see me for a couple of minutes?"

● "I was so excited about the job opportunity you advertised in the *Journal* that I drove over as fast as possible. I really think I'd be perfect for that job! Is there any chance I might speak with someone about it while I'm here?"

● If you're in a smaller business and you can actually see a decision-maker, say, "I realize I don't have an appointment, but I really think I'd be perfect for the job you're advertising. Could we spend a couple of minutes discussing it?"

● If you're visiting, even if you're not aware of a specific job opening, say, "I wonder if I might fill out an application and leave my resume.... Do you suppose someone would be willing to speak with me for a couple of minutes about possible future job opportunities?" If you spot an apparent decision-maker, say, "My name is Mary Smith. I'm in the job market and I'm particularly interested in your company. I know you probably don't have any immediate openings, but would you be willing to spend five minutes sharing some ideas on how someone like me should approach the job market?"

Certainly, there is no guarantee that visiting will lead to an interview, but the strategy is as old as selling. If you are pleasant and professional and you ask enough people, you'll eventually find a person who just learned that a key employee is leaving, a person who has been halfway thinking about a new hire, or even a person who respects your moxie and will spend a few minutes with you.

Unconventional Mail Follow-Up

> *"Only your imagination limits the number of methods of recontacting a target company."*

Only your imagination limits the number of methods of recontacting a target company. As a very basic unconventional approach, you can simply develop a set of letters or cards designed strictly to keep your name in front of the decision-maker:

- "In reflecting further on your job opportunity, I became even more convinced that my abilities fit your needs. During my three years at ABC Corp., I created 24 new accounts of the type your company is seeking. My resume may not make clear the extent to which our new client program fits your objectives. I am excited about pursuing this opportunity and look forward to hearing from you soon."

- "My resume is presently on file with you. I worked hard to keep it to one page, but in reflecting on your job opportunity, I realized that I left off some very relevant experience…"

- If your experience is limited versus other likely candidates, write, "I woke up this morning with the really bad feeling that my resume may not be on the top of your stack. I know there are other applicants with a longer list of jobs, but I truly feel you'll be making the right decision if you give me an interview. I know enough to hit the ground running in the job. What I don't know immediately, I'll learn quickly. And you'll never find someone who will work harder to make the job and your company successful…. Thanks in advance for your consideration."

Many applicants orchestrate a campaign including as many as three follow-up mailings, a phone call, and appropriate "thank-you" mailings after the interviews. Examples of less-conventional mail follow-up include the following:

- Create a truly unusual version of your resume, as discussed in chapter 9.

- A follow-up letter can include something unique, such as a gag reference list with testimonials:

    "He certainly knows how to save pennies so that his company increases earnings." —Benjamin Franklin

    "He works harder to develop good ideas than I did when I invented the light bulb." —Thomas Edison

    The list should include some quotations from recognized historical figures in the industry—a subtle way to demonstrate knowledge.

Using the unusual can certainly fulfill the goal of making your application a "keeper." It is certain that a person who receives a wildly unique resume will react strongly. If they're the kind of people who react positively to initiative and creativity, you leap ahead of competitive applications.

Whether using the usual or the unusual, the follow-up concept completes your job-search strategy. You have a resume, a tailored cover letter, and a preplanned set of follow-up steps. As you relentlessly execute this strategy, good things are much more likely to happen.

Fit Your Campaign to the Hiring Process

Note the importance of becoming aware of the target company's hiring procedure. Many companies, particularly large businesses, have a multi-step process that might include the following:

- Prescreening to 40 applicants by a human resources clerk

- Prescreening to 15 applicants by a human resources manager

- Screening to six interviewees by the working manager

- First interview for the top six

- Second interview for the top three

If you can understand this process in advance, learn the names of key people, and execute follow-up with the right people along the way, your odds increase dramatically.

The other extreme is a small company in which the entrepreneur is also the personnel department. He is likely very busy. His hiring system is something like this:

- Quickly read through the resume stack.

- Find three or four that look good.

- Call 'em in.

- Hire the first who really seems to fit the need.

In the 21st-century job market, a very large percentage of job openings are being created in the small business sector. Fortunately, the entire Edge concept fits extremely well with a small-business, entrepreneurial mentality that tends to appreciate initiative and creativity.

Every element of this book can be brought to bear in this kind of job search. You can conduct your research of available opportunities by aggressively reading and networking. Once you find an attractive company, you can continue your research at two specific levels:

- The company's business situation and needs

- The CEO's individual background, style, and interests

A unique campaign will likely be noticed and appreciated. It is possible to directly approach the CEO with suggestions such as "I am confident I'm your person for this manufacturing job. Let me visit your company at my own expense for two days. I'll just observe and then give you a report on my observations and recommendations. I believe you'll see I have the kind of knowledge and skills you're looking for. If not, I'm history."

Using the Fax

Communication by fax offers another Edge opportunity. You can fax a resume early on Monday morning with the note "I wanted to be your first response to the job opportunity listed in _____ . My actual resume will follow by mail."

You can re-create your own fax transmittal form as a demonstration of creativity. And the fax offers another means for unique follow-up.

Mastering the Interview

"John, do you really think he's tough enough for a good practice interview?"

Although the scope of this book does not include in-depth coverage of the interviewing process, it's a subject that's too important to omit. Chasing interviews without being fully prepared for those interviews seems akin to the dog that chases cars. What in the world does he do with it if he catches it?

This chapter covers some fundamentals of the interviewing process and provides references for additional study and preparation.

Applying the Edge Philosophy to Your Interviewing Style

Some have asked whether we feel the Edge concept of "daring to be different" should be stretched into the interviewing process. As with all elements of the Edge concept, you have to make decisions about when and where you can use them most effectively. In deciding when to apply Edge techniques to the interview process, you need to assess your current status and your competitive qualifications.

For example, if your Edge resume has brought you successfully through a major screening process and you have reason to believe you are very competitive in terms of qualifications, personal traits, and interviewing technique, it seems unduly risky to adopt unconventional interviewing tactics.

However, if your Edge resume has helped you secure an interview against heavy odds (and this happens frequently), you face the same dilemma in the interviewing process that you faced with the resume: The competitors are likely to have a "better pedigree" in terms of direct experience. It makes no sense to ignore the likely disadvantage you face. Therefore, your interview must directly, skillfully address your likely shortcomings. Using the Edge philosophy, you confidently state that you're aware of—and fully prepared to conquer—the perceived disadvantages you may face going into the job. Examples of appropriate comments might be the following:

- "I believe experience is important; certainly, a person must be well-grounded in the fundamentals of our business. But there are people with so much experience that they've quit questioning, quit learning, quit growing. I feel fully ready to take on this job—and I'll be the kind of person who will never stand still. I'll grow as much as it's possible to grow in the job—and I'll look forward to whatever other positions the company allows me to tackle."

- "I am confident I have all the technical skills it takes to handle this job. And I'll bring the kind of positive attitude, enthusiasm, and work ethic that can really help energize my department. When I was at Acme, I was able to generate a 12 percent increase in productivity—partly because I implemented new systems, but mainly because I instilled a 'roll up your sleeves and get the job done' attitude, which turned my department around."

- "I suppose there will be a few technical things I won't know the day I start—but I sure won't stand around feeling stupid. I am an aggressive learner. I find the people who know the answers, and I learn from them. I find the right books and articles and take the right courses. In other words, within days, not weeks, I'll be fully informed about every aspect of that position. And I'll keep growing from there!"

It is vitally important that your interviewing style be totally comfortable—the "real you" rather than an attempt to play a role. Therefore, whether your approach is rather conservative or more aggressive, it must fit your personality. At the same time, it's vital to…

> "*Chasing interviews without being fully prepared for those interviews seems akin to the dog that chases cars. What in the world does he do with it if he catches it?*"

Practice, Practice, Practice

It is a strange trait of human nature that we will spend significant time in rehearsal for minor speeches to minor organizations, but we tend to "wing it" when it comes to job interviews.

In fact, for most of us, becoming comfortable in the interviewing process requires a great deal of practice.

One excellent technique is asking a friend to play interviewer to your interviewee. Request tough questions in random order. If possible, videotape your performance to watch for verbal slips (uh, um, ya know, uh, um) and any unpleasant nervous habits.

Of course, real interviews are the best practice—and the more you do, the better. If possible, be like the young boy who asked a hostile girl to the dance. "Tom, why did you ask Nancy? You knew she'd say no." "I know, but I wanted to practice my asking so Melissa might say yes." A couple of practice interviews for jobs you don't really want can be ideal practice for the really crucial interview.

Asking the *Right* Questions

As we discussed in chapter 3, it is vital that you go into an interview with as much specific knowledge about the company as possible. The more you know, the better you'll be able to ask the right questions during the interview. Of course, the best way to start is to do your research. By now, the map of your library should be permanently etched on your brain. Also, get out on the Internet and review the company's Web site, online industry publications, and other published resources. Read, take notes, study! Use the worksheet on page 163 to organize the information you gather. Be prepared to ask intelligent questions, such as those shown on the next page.

Asking questions such as these will serve to impress the interviewer as well as provide you with valuable information. Be aware, however, of a possible hidden agenda when an interviewer asks

Sample Questions to Ask During an Interview

▶ What are the day-to-day responsibilities of the person in this position?

▶ Why is this position open? Where is the person now who was previously in this position?

▶ What is a potential career path beginning with this position in the company?

▶ Exactly where does this position fit into the overall organizational structure of the company?

▶ Are there important changes, such as expansion of products or services, that will affect my position?

▶ Are the procedures of the position set in stone, or is a person encouraged to contribute innovative ideas?

if you have any questions: If your set of questions is simplistic, it tips off the interviewer that you are very green or very unfamiliar with basic information about the company or industry.

Also, be aware that initiating conversation regarding salary and benefits during the first interview could harm your chances for a second interview. Some interviewers feel that early discussion of money is a clue that a person is focused on "What's in it for me?" rather than being a dedicated professional.

Some Interviewing Fundamentals

The time is here, and you have arrived at your interview destination 10 to 15 minutes early. You allowed the extra time to ensure against traffic problems and to give yourself a few minutes in the rest room to be sure everything is groomed, tucked in, and zipped. Your dress is conservative, and appropriate as best you understand it for the kind of job for which you're applying. You have attended to the small details that some interviewers study carefully: shoes polished, nails in good shape, little or no perfume or aftershave.

> *"You allowed the extra time to ensure against traffic problems and…to be sure everything is groomed, tucked in, and zipped."*

Because you may be meeting with more than one interviewer, you've brought along several extra resumes. You have pen, paper, and calculator in an impressive case or binder. You are prepared to complete an application form, with relevant dates of education, employment, and military service. You have names, addresses, and phone numbers of previous employers and references. If appropriate, you've brought along a portfolio of relevant accomplishments from previous jobs or recent educational programs.

The Interview Begins

You have taken whatever steps you need to take to overcome the biggest enemy: nervousness. Being relaxed is doubly crucial. A nervous candidate obviously does not exude the confidence people seek in an employee. Even worse, nervousness can shut down the mind and affect the voice—not the desired physical response for good interviewing.

Excellent preparation is critical. If you have studied the company, know more about the situation than competitive candidates, and have practiced your questions and answers, you can relax with the knowledge that you're well out in front of most applicants.

And don't forget: The interviewer is just another human. In fact, many interviewers are uncomfortable with the process and are hopeful that there will be a "click" between personalities that will make the interview more pleasant. If it can be done gracefully, try to find some pre-interview bonding topics—kids, family, vacations, and college experiences—to create a more pleasant relationship. Scanning the walls and desks for pictures, diplomas, or trip mementos might give you clues.

Generating a laugh can help, but joking is risky until you have a clue that the interviewer has a sense of humor. If so, you can probably generate a thawing chuckle with lines such as

- "Do you mind if I sit over there (his chair)? I hate this side of the desk."

- "It must be grim interviewing a bunch of people. Do you ever want to record your questions and just go golfing?"

During the Interview

As the interview progresses, you need to be alert to questions and feedback, but you also need to be aware of how you're coming across to your interviewer. Remember these basics:

- Eye contact is crucial. Many applicants sink immediately because poor eye contact makes them seem shifty.

- Answers should be kept under two minutes each. Be very sensitive to clues that you are talking too much. Some interviewers begin fidgeting, glancing around the room, or checking their watches. Some might yawn. In the worst example we've ever heard, one applicant reported that his interviewer actually dozed off.

- Exaggeration is risky. Good interviewers make mental or written notes and often check references to verify answers.

- On the other hand, amplify answers to include information that sells your skills and accomplishments. For example, in response to a question about the number of people you've managed at one time, "As Sales Manager at ABC Products, I was responsible for hiring, training, and managing as many as 15 sales representatives covering 4 states. My team exceeded quota by 75 percent during the three years I was there, so I feel my approach to management and motivation was very effective."

- Avoid speaking negatively about anything, particularly your previous position, company, or boss. Many interviewers are simply turned off by negatives. Others will conclude

153

that the negatives are a clue that you are a griper and complainer.

- Be sure to ask the interviewer what the next set of steps will be. His answer will probably give a strong clue regarding your status after the interview. "Well, uh, someone will be in touch" is much less promising than "We'll conduct follow-up interviews next week, and I expect you'll be contacted."

- Follow up the interview with a letter or handwritten thank-you note that ties to the balance of the application process. "Thanks for the opportunity to meet with you. I'm looking forward to meeting with Mr. Sandifer next week. I'm more convinced than ever that this position represents an excellent career step, and I'm hopeful you agree that my qualifications fit your requirements."

- Finally, take advantage of the Interview Follow-Up Worksheet on page 166 to gather your thoughts in one place after the interview.

Additional References

At any bookstore or online book source, you can find a number of good publications that deal with interviewing techniques. These references have been consulted by many Edge associates:

Farr, J. Michael. *The Quick Interview and Salary Negotiation Book.* JIST Works, Inc., 8902 Otis Avenue, Indianapolis, IN 46216. 1995.

Porto, Daniel and Frances Bolles Haynes. *101 Toughest Interview Questions and Answers That Win the Job!* Ten Speed Press, Box 7123, Berkeley, CA 94707. 1999.

Yate, Martin J. *Knock 'Em Dead 1999 with Great Answers to Tough Interview Questions.* Bob Adams, Holbrook, MA 02343. 1999.

Yeager, Neil M. and Lee Hough. *Power Interviews: Job-Winning Tactics from Fortune 500 Recruiters.* John Wiley & Sons, 605 Third Avenue, New York, NY 10158-0012. 1998.

Interview Questions You May Be Asked

Job interviews can take as many different directions as there are people conducting the interviews. However, most interviews will touch upon some common themes at some point. Here is a list of questions that interviewers frequently ask:

1. Tell me about yourself.

2. Why should I hire you?

3. Why are you looking for a new job?

4. Why did you leave your previous position?

5. Have you ever been fired from a job? Why?

6. What did you like most about your previous position?

7. What did you like least about your previous position?

8. Why do you want this position?

9. What other positions are you interviewing for?

10. What do you want from a job?

11. How would you describe the ideal job?

12. Why did you choose this career path?

13. What are your greatest strengths? Greatest weaknesses?

14. Where do you see yourself five years from now? Ten years from now?

15. What are some of your short-term goals?

16. What are some of your long-term goals?

17. Tell me about a goal you set for yourself recently and how you accomplished it.

18. What two or three accomplishments have given you the most satisfaction?

19. How do you determine or evaluate success?

20. What is the worst mistake you have ever made on the job? How did you remedy the problem?

21. What is a major problem that you have encountered, and how did you deal with it?

22. What have you learned from your mistakes?

23. What motivates you?

24. How do you go about making important decisions?

25. If you could change something about your life, what would it be?

26. What activities are you involved in? What are your hobbies?

27. What have you learned from participation in activities away from your job/career?

28. What is the last book you read? What is the last movie you saw?

29. What do you know about this company?

30. What do you think a company should provide its employees?

31. What criteria are you using to evaluate the company you hope to work for?

32. What do you think it takes to be successful in a company like ours?

33. In what ways do you think you can make a contribution to our company?

34. What qualities should a successful manager possess?

35. Tell me about the best boss you ever had. The worst.

36. How well do you work under pressure?

37. How do you think a friend who knows you well would describe you? How do you think a former associate/ colleague would describe you?

38. What is your best friend like? What does he or she do?

39. Do you consider yourself a leader or a follower? Why?

40. Do you prefer working with others or by yourself? Why?

41. What type of personality is the most difficult for you to get along with?

42. Why did you choose the college you attended?

43. Why didn't you attend college?

44. How and why did you choose your major?

45. What college subjects did you like best? Why?

46. How was your college education funded?

47. How many days of work did you miss in your last position?

48. How long do you plan on staying in your next position?

49. How do you feel about travel? Locally? Nationally? Internationally? How many days out of the year are acceptable?

50. How do you feel about relocation?

51. Has anyone made you an offer yet? If so, why haven't you accepted? If not, why not?

52. What are you currently earning?

53. How much do you feel you are worth? How much do you want to be earning?

CHAPTER

12

Step-by-Step Action Plan Worksheets

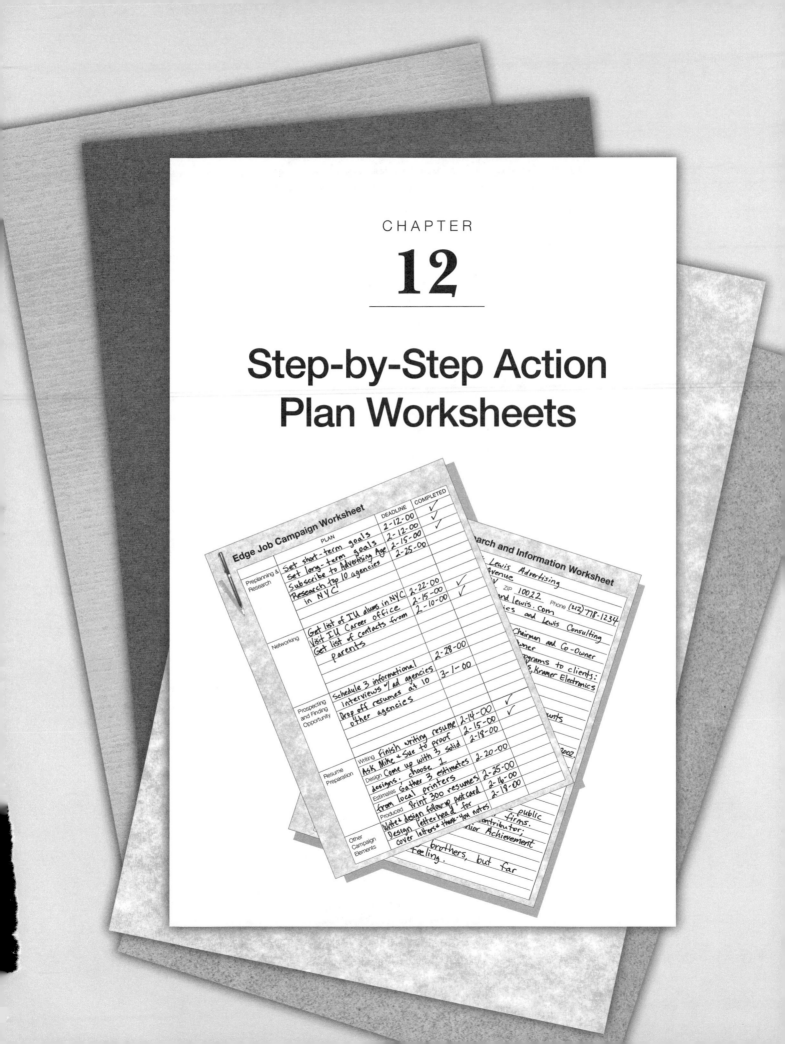

Effectively executing the Edge strategy requires careful organization of a job-search campaign. As we discussed in chapter 10, using the Edge strategy requires more than just randomly mailing resumes and hoping for the best. Although it involves more effort, the Edge strategy is also much more effective.

It's important to carefully organize the components of your campaign. The following pages provide forms that might be helpful. You are free to reproduce these forms or to modify the designs to better fit your needs.

The forms include

- An overall master plan, including target and actual timetables

- A research form for logging information about individual companies

- A networking form for logging contacts and leads

- A marketing form for logging your outgoing mailings

- An interview form for detailing progress with companies who have responded to your initial contact

These thumbnails show sample uses of each form:

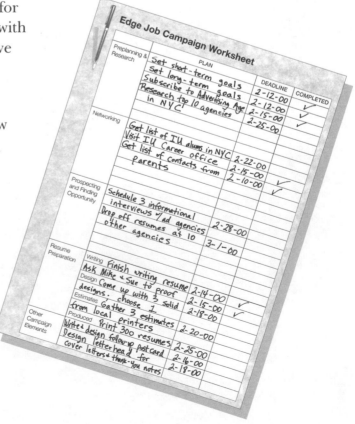

Company Research and Information Worksheet

Company Name Lewis & Lewis Advertising
Address 524 Third Avenue   Phone (212) 778-1234
City New York   State NY   ZIP 10022
Web Site Address www.lewisandlewis.com
Subsidiaries/Divisions Lewis Graphics and Lewis Consulting
Names of Key Personnel Thomas Lewis, Chairman and Co-Owner
Brad Lewis, President and Co-Owner
Products/Services Sales of advertising programs to clients:
(major) Dome Services, Butler Foods, Kramer Electronics

Financial Condition stable and growing
Gross Sales Last Year approx. 5.2 million
Plans for Expansion—Building or Employees depending on a
secured or lost, employees come and go;
turnover remains low.
Goals of the Company Financially- to reach
Would like to expand into new and mo
advertising designs.
Competitors of the Company Poster Companie
Comm quo Company.

Ranking in the Industry 22nd largest in
Company's Public Image not too visibl
because of the popularity of t
Community Involvement Major United W
participating sponsor for

Employee Turnover Rate low
Organizational Structure run by
from a family fee

Networking Contacts Worksheet

DATE	NAME/TITLE/COMPANY	ADDRESS/PHONE/E-MAIL	REFERRED BY	ACTION PLAN
2-10-00	Tom Miller Graphic Artist LN Saatchi+Saatchi	767 Fifth Ave. NY, NY 10022 (212) 755-0060 tmiller@lautrecn.com	friend of mine	Call him by 2-13-00. He referred me to Marilyn Hiatt.
2-10-00	Helen McConnell VP, Marketing, WNTS	1800 N. Meridian Indpls, IN 46204 (317) 636-0000 hmcconnell@wnts.com	former associate of mom's	Call her by 2-14-00. Meeting her for lunch 2-17-00.

Marketing Worksheet

COMPANY/ADDRESS	CONTACT PERSON	POSITION PURSUED	ACTION TAKEN	DATE	STAT
The Interpublic Group, Inc. 1271 Ave. of the Americas New York, NY 10020 (212) 399-8000	Diane Scott Regional Acct. Manager	Advertising Account Exec	Mailed resume	2-15-00	no
			Mailed post card	2-21-00	no
			Called Diane Scott	2-25-00	int 3-

Interview Follow-Up Worksheet

Company Name Lautrec Nazca Saatchi & Saatchi
Address 767 Fifth Avenue   Phone (212) 755-0060
City New York   State NY   ZIP 10022
Position Advertising Account Executive
Source Tom Miller, Graphic Artist for S+S, friend
Job Description Responsible for calling on new & old
companies within assigned area. Promote S+S to
potential clients. Service established clients. Report
with weekly & monthly sales reports and
customer status.
Requirements Strong advertising sales experience, esp.
in food and beverage products. Desire to travel
within the state. Excellent written & verbal
skills. Ability to motivate self & client.
Contact Person Marilyn Hiatt, Regional Account Manager
Interviewers
Marilyn Hiatt, Reg. Acct. Mgr.
David McDonald, VP Adv. Sales   Status   Thank You Sent
Jeff Coffman, SVP Adv. Sls   Interview 4/2   Interview 4/23   yes   Interview 5/11   yes

Notes & Feelings Great rapport with Marilyn. David
introduced me to 4 other Acct. Execs. All
seem to have good feelings about teamwork.
Need to reiterate my skills in a note to David. He
seemed preoccupied during the interview. So far I
like the atmosphere & responsibilities. If the
money is right, I'll take it.

Attach newspaper advertisement if applicable.

Edge Job Campaign Worksheet

	PLAN	DEADLINE	COMPLETED
Preplanning & Research			
Networking			
Prospecting and Finding Opportunity			
Resume Preparation	Writing		
	Design		
	Estimates		
	Produced		
Other Campaign Elements			

This form may be photocopied for personal use. It may not be resold.

Company Research and Information Worksheet

Company Name _____

Address _____

City _____ State _____ ZIP _____ Phone _____

Web Site Address _____

Subsidiaries/Divisions _____

_____

Names of Key Personnel _____

_____

Products/Services _____

_____

_____

Financial Condition _____

Gross Sales Last Year _____

Plans for Expansion—Building or Employees _____

_____

_____

Goals of the Company _____

_____

_____

Competitors of the Company _____

_____

_____

Ranking in the Industry _____

Company's Public Image _____

_____

Community Involvement _____

_____

_____

Employee Turnover Rate _____

Organizational Structure _____

_____

This form may be photocopied for personal use. It may not be resold.

Networking Contacts Worksheet

DATE	NAME/TITLE/COMPANY	ADDRESS/PHONE/E-MAIL	REFERRED BY	ACTION PLAN

This form may be photocopied for personal use. It may not be resold.

Marketing Worksheet

COMPANY/ADDRESS	CONTACT PERSON	POSITION PURSUED	ACTION TAKEN	DATE	STATUS

This form may be photocopied for personal use. It may not be resold.

Interview Follow-Up Worksheet

Company Name _____

Address _____

City _____ State _____ ZIP _____ Phone _____

Position _____

Source _____

Job Description _____

_____

_____

_____

_____

Requirements _____

_____

_____

_____

_____

_____

Contact Person _____

Interviewers	Status	Thank-You Sent
_____	_____	_____
_____	_____	_____
_____	_____	_____
_____	_____	_____
_____	_____	_____
_____	_____	_____

Notes & Feelings _____

_____

_____

_____

_____

_____

_____

Attach newspaper advertisement if applicable.